FLÂNEUR

FLÂNEUR

The Art of Wandering the Streets of Paris

FEDERICO CASTIGLIANO

© 2017 Federico Castigliano

ISBN-13: 978-1546942092
ISBN-10: 1546942092

federicocastigliano.com
facebook.com/intothestreet

All rights reserved. No portion of this book may be reproduced in any form without written permission.

CreateSpace Independent Publishing Platform
North Charleston, South Carolina
Graphic design and cover: Isaia Pruneddu
ezds.co

Second English edition, revised and expanded, 2017

Table of contents

	Itineraries of flânerie	11
0.	Instructions for reading this book	13
1.	Prologue – Into the street *Rive Droite*	15
2.	How to be a true flâneur	21
3.	A day in the life of a flâneur *Rive Gauche*	28
4.	Once there was the flâneur	51
5.	Getting lost *Opéra, Rue Saint-Denis*	61
6.	Where to wander in Paris *The Seine, Palais-Royal, Montmartre*	70
7.	Drifting along the boulevards *Grands Boulevards*	79
8.	The ruins of Paris	87
9.	A dangerous game *Pont Neuf*	93
10.	The city of tomorrow *Tour Eiffel, Disneyland Paris*	103
11.	Shopping as one of the fine arts *La Défense*	112

12.	Paris spleen *Boulevard de Bonne-Nouvelle*	121
13.	Epilogue – At the gate *Charles de Gaulle Airport*	128
	Memorandum for flâneurs	136
	Bibliography	139
	About the author	151

Flâneur: an idle man-about-town

(Merriam-Webster Dictionary)

Itineraries of flânerie

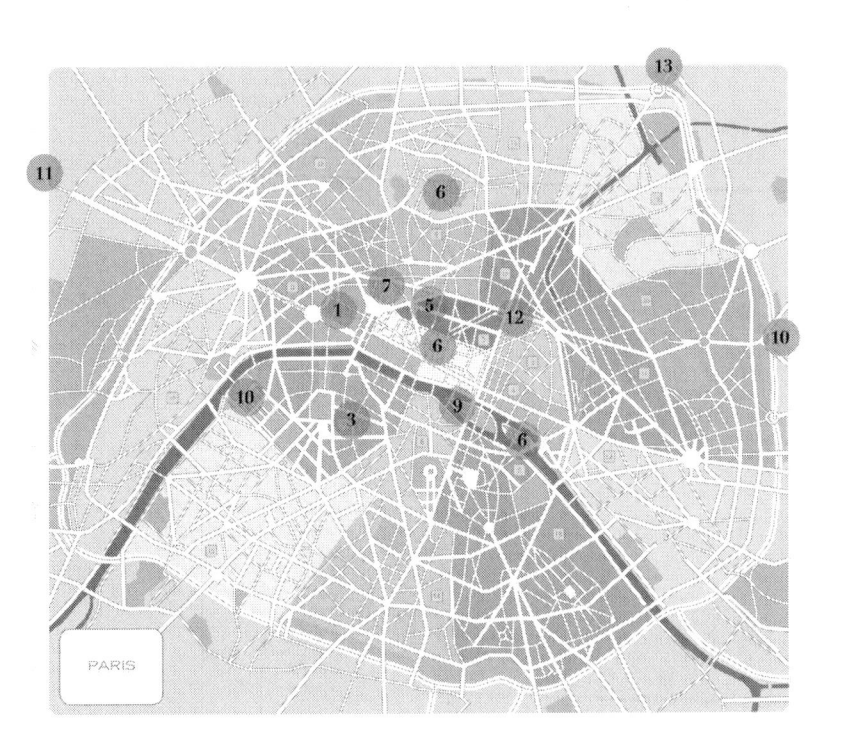

0.

Instructions for reading this book

This book teaches how to wander aimlessly, how to get lost in the city. It is dedicated to those who are never sated, those incessantly amazed by the beauty of the world. Reading these pages will initiate you into flânerie: you will learn how to transform a simple walk through the streets of Paris into an exciting and memorable experience.

The result of years of study, of walks and adventures, *Flâneur* seeks to suggest new ways of living and experiences guiding the reader through a deeper and direct knowledge of Paris. You will find here some tales about *promenades* and urban exploration, stories of dandies and flâneurs, of people who have lost their way and others who have discovered new and wonderful things on their journey. You will find information about historical personages, authors and artists who have made the history of urban walking – a literary and cultural tradition developed over the course of two centuries with special relevance to the city of Paris. You will also find some ideas and suggestions for a creative and novel use of the city and its spaces. This book can be looked upon as an alternative guide, a manual designed both for travellers and for Parisians, for those who don't want to conform to mass culture and tourism.

A book dealing with flânerie, this noble art of wandering the streets of Paris, certainly cannot be organized entirely as a novel, nor as a systematic treatise. The structure of *Flâneur* allows for two opposing ways of reading it: a conventional, sequential way, from the first to the last chapter, or more freely, adopting a flâneur-like attitude that leaves the reader at liberty to trace a preferred route within the text. All you have to bear in mind is a simple rule: the chapters with odd numbers are fiction, while the chapters with even numbers are nonfiction. Each chapter is independent in meaning, and yet is linked to the others thanks to a series of correspondences and references. Even the positioning of the prologue and the epilogue could, ultimately, be inverted. The introduction to the setting at the beginning of each chapter adds another key to reading the book, this time spatial and geographical. Readers indeed can decide to first consult the map and then read at their convenience and in any order the chapters dedicated to the Parisian *arrondissements* they wish to visit.

1.

Prologue - Into the street

Rive Droite

Sometimes, when the symphony of the city has been knocking at my door from early in the morning, I descend into the street, wrapped in my black overcoat, and set off along the bustling avenues of the Right Bank. These are the gloomy days of winter when Parisian melancholy torments the soul and provokes free spirits into a long-lasting drift with no purpose and no destination. I have no appointments; I do not have any specific goal in mind. I wander aimlessly through the tentacular city. Yet, although determined to travel purely at random, I seem almost to be following some railway track, a pre-ordained route, with no deviations. So I end up covering the entire stretch of the boulevards, several times – from République to Madeleine, Madeleine to République. Through the fog, I look at the pale façades and shop windows that line the street. I contemplate the stuccoes and wrought-iron balconies. The austere elevations of the Boulevard Haussmann. Then, when feverish and numbed by the cold and the neon lights, I take refuge under the dome of the Galeries Lafayette.

Paris is narcotic for a man alone, a never-ending labyrinth where the anxiety of freedom is relieved. The city appears like a series of sets, in which every sequence is connected to another by a fine thread, and the whole comes together to create a coherent film. On the hallowed territory of the city, walking has become, for me, an ascetic ritual. For this reason, when I am carried away by a sudden urge or struck by an apparition – a distant sign, the swish of a skirt or a falling leaf – I leave the main road and traipse the streets adjoining the boulevards. I wander through the faded alleys of the Sentier, through the fine art auctions, towards Drouot, but mainly in the triangle bounded by Rue Saint-Augustin, Rue de Richelieu and Avenue de l'Opéra – that Far Eastern oasis centered around Rue Sainte-Anne, my own "little Tokyo".

Paris, we know, is no longer the center of the world, but it is the perfect place to consecrate yourself to your own vices and, in my case, that typical Parisian habit which is to spend my days wandering about, with no end result. In the city, the intimacy of the "villages" alternate with great nineteenth-century boulevards, lined with bar and restaurant terraces, where people sit as if in the cinema, watching life go by. Thanks to the abundance and variety of its monuments and its dense, uninterrupted urban fabric, but also due to its uniquely interpenetrating public and private spaces, Paris is made to be walked. In this respect, the French capital differs from metropolises of more recent origin, such as those in emerging countries, but also from other European cities with an artistic heritage: it was right here – rather than in Florence or Rome – that the art of wandering the city streets developed, finding expression in a rich cultural and literary tradition.

The figure of the solitary walking man, observing the landscape of the city and its crowds, made its appearance in French art and literature towards the middle of the nineteenth century. The term "flâneur" was used, in fact, to indicate a type of individual, usually an intellectual or artist, who strolled aimlessly around a Paris that was undergoing profound architectural and social transformation. Free and alone in the maze of the city, the flâneur craves a revelation that might change his life and destiny. He seeks to capture and eventually to preserve, through artistic or literary expression, a new form of beauty, in accordance with the aesthetic criteria that were in the process of being defined in modern European culture. Thus, if the establishment of metropolitan environments has influenced the history of literature and the arts of the modern era, it is precisely through artistic and literary works that a particular image of the city has been "constructed", assigning symbolic meaning to its physical forms and inventing different ways of using and interpreting its spaces. The interplay between literature and reality evokes the metaphor of the city as a text or semiotic structure. The city appears to the flâneur as something intelligible, a "plot", a story that can be told.

During the years I spent in Paris, I too was a flâneur. I sought to explore more or less systematically every arrondissement, every neighborhood of the French capital. I tried to learn the names of the roads by heart, to remember the precise sequence of the façades of the buildings along a boulevard. I sought to observe the changes in mood of a square in the various moments of the day, in the four seasons, under different skies. And I tied the facts of my life so tightly to the spaces of the city, to the point that every corner of Paris reminds me of a conversation with a friend, an episode, a love. I know that many people use the streets of the city as a space to be crossed quickly in order to go from one place to another and get their business done. But my story, the one I am about to recount, is quite different. The first time I met Paris – and I'm not referring to the first time I visited the city as a tourist, but the first time I found myself alone and naked before it –, that day Paris was for me an exciting mystery. And then, gradually, I learned to get to know the city more profoundly, to move through it, to study its past, and our relationship became more intimate. Paris became part of me, but I am also part, in some way, of Paris.

Many years have gone by and although the circumstances of my life have taken me far away, I still occasionally close my eyes and imagine a walk through Paris. Now that there is also a mental distance between me and this city, I wonder what remains of all that time spent walking like a madman, of that confused but passionate quest for a truth that I thought was inscribed on the façades of the buildings, entrapped in the atmosphere of a neighborhood. What remains, in the end, of a love? Of all the enterprises that one may attempt, of all the activities to which one can consecrate one's energies and youth, flânerie is certainly among the most useless. The flâneur, by definition, is going nowhere. To become expert in the art of flânerie you have to study carefully the history of the city, train your eye, develop memory and orientation, reinforce your physical stamina. But your training as a flâneur can have no professional opening, it leads neither to a successful career nor to celebrity. Balzac said that flânerie is a science, the "gastronomy of the eye"; but it is a science that, for the moment, has no academy or official recognition.

I have long been seduced by the idea of losing myself, persuaded by the thought that there was something poetic in this dissipation. I thought that the destiny of every true flâneur was to immerse himself in the panorama surrounding him, to the point of becoming one with it and, ultimately, to vanish. To listen to the voice of the world, the self must be silenced. And the flâneur is the incarnation of this ideal: dazzled by beauty, he decides to relinquish the self in order to consecrate his life to contemplation. Lost in the maze of the city, he progressively sheds all the teaching received and adheres to the visible reality like a chameleon. The man who wanders in the city projects himself on the façades of the buildings, on the shop windows sparkling in their sequence, on the faces of the people who pass by. It is precisely this ability to annul oneself, to come out from the stifling prison of the inner life, this is the science and the skill of the flâneur. "Not finding the road that you are looking for," – said Walter Benjamin, the writer who initiated the study of flânerie at the beginning of the twentieth century – "does not mean much. But to lose one's way in the city, as one loses one's way in a forest, requires some schooling."[1]

---

[1] Whoever decides to study the historical, social and cultural origins of the flâneur, is obliged to venture into treacherous territory, on the boundaries between literary criticism, urban studies and sociology. The posthumous publication of *Das Passagen-Werk* (1982), the collection of notes in which Walter Benjamin considered the flâneur as a representative figure of the modern era, did indeed instigate a stream of particularly fruitful studies, to the point that reference to the practice of flânerie spread, starting in the 1990s, in literary studies as well as in social sciences, relating to disparate disciplines. Despite all this, the flâneur remains an indistinct and elusive character who offers some resistance to those attempting to classify him in prevalently theoretical discourse.

2.

How to be a true flâneur

To be a true flâneur you must first forget every commonplace, ignore the banalities and the mundane things seen on television or read in the newspapers. The flâneur must be himself in the city just as the first man was himself before Nature. To his gaze the city appears as a grand spectacle without purpose, without meaning. Paris presents itself to the flâneur as the realm of the possible, the ideal place in which all experiences are theoretically achievable. In exploring a city, some prefer to follow a maniacal scheme, visiting roads or monuments in alphabetical order, moving around with a compass or with a pedometer. Others love to follow in a prosaic manner the instructions of tourist guides, or the suggestions they have heard from friends or acquaintances. Nevertheless, although it may appear paradoxical, in order to acquire a profound view of things, you must first of all move randomly. This is the founding dogma and, I would dare say, the "gnoseological principle" of flânerie.

The flâneur moves through the city with neither a map nor a plan. He has to feel himself to be free and alone, ready and willing for the imponderable. The attitude of the true flâneur consists of not establishing a hierarchy between what most people consider important and what instead, normally, is not of any interest to anyone. There exists a mysterious energy in chance, a secret correspondence that connects the elements of the outside world with the inner being of the walking man. It is therefore indispensable to push oneself towards ever-new realities, to do that which the ordinary person, normally, would never do. One can, eyes closed, put a finger on the map and take oneself off to an unknown place. Or choose an underground or bus station completely randomly and explore the area in which it sits. The suburbs, wastelands or building sites are not to be neglected. River paths must be followed, airports and the great railway stations visited. The leaves on the trees, the greater or lesser flow of cars along a road, must be observed. Consecrate oneself to the reading of the faces and the gaits of passers-by.

At this point let us clear up a fundamental question: flânerie is not to be confused hastily with tourism, nor with the pathetic coming and going along the city streets. It would be ingenuous to think that. It would be puerile to believe that a simple walk along the Champs-Elysées might be defined as a flânerie. Most people are completely incapable of walking without a destination and exploring the undersides of a city. It is difficult to find a true flâneur, i.e. a person capable of freeing himself from the chain of material requirements and needs to the point of acquiring a vision of the world that is not strictly functional. Only the flâneur is able to establish an intimate relationship with the city that leads him to adapt his own mood, his own interior being, to that of the place. The city belongs to the flâneur, but the flâneur becomes, in his turn, part of the city. There is something of him that remains, like a shadow, on the sculpted stone, on the pavements of the roads he walks along. The city is the home and territory of the flâneur. Along the boulevards of Paris, the crowds tire themselves among the shops – harried, loaded with anxiety and bags, while the flâneur walks lightly and observes the urban scene, almost ecstatic. His gaze encompasses a wider-ranging reality than that of the common man.

But at times there is something febrile, sick, in the flâneur's gait. He wanders through the city, seems to be on a quest for a chimera. His destination is confused or is unattainable. His steps become nervous, exasperated: he looks like a man on the run. The flâneur flees from the ordinariness of common life. He flees from the memories and the ghosts of his own interior. The glowing phenomenal appearance fills the empty cavity of his ego. The flâneur is a man cast out onto the street by a restlessness, by an impatience for the quest that haunts him and sets him apart from those who remain seated at tables simply enjoying their coffee. The flâneur wanders restless through the city like an untamed beast. He succumbs to the crowd like a wreck to the waves, letting himself be overcome by the liberating breath of anarchy. There is something voluptuous, almost orgiastic, in this dissolution.

The flâneur is he who consecrates his own life to the instant, to ephemeral things. The treasures he searches for exist for a brief moment, but then, like spectacular butterflies, they fly away. Of the atmosphere he savors so enthusiastically today, tomorrow nothing will remain. The flâneur aspires to ubiquity, but there is always some detail, some aspect of the world that eludes him. His regret is in not being able to see all that is visible, not being able to live all imaginable experiences. You cannot enjoy a beautiful sunset simultaneously from the Sacré Coeur and from the top of the Tour Montparnasse. You cannot love two women at the same time. From the disparity between the immensity of the possible and the smallness of the human being there springs the torment and the energy of the flâneur. Persecuted by frustration, he is sentenced to a sort of perpetual motion.

There are some flâneurs who do nothing more than walk like madmen and use up all their energy in the simple gesture of wandering and observing. These are pure flâneurs. Others, instead, seek to attribute a further sense to their walking and cultivate artistic ambitions. The flâneur deludes himself into thinking that the beauty of the world might contain a message, something profound and ineffable for most people. Creative activity is thus an attempt to freeze the moment, to block the chaos. With a photograph one seeks to transform an instant into the eternal. With a novel one seeks to trace a destiny, to attribute a higher sense to the random flow of events of which he is spectator. The flâneur is an author in search of his characters and his intrigue. Music too can be born of flânerie, if the steps of the walking man manage to fall into time with the melody of the city, with the urban rhythm. With its noises, with its silences.

Let us now consider the physical side of the flâneur. Walking ceaselessly, especially in the rainy and unwholesome climate of Paris, requires good physical shape. You have to go several hours without eating and without resting. The flâneur is an ascetic who manages to ignore things lacking in importance and to concentrate on what is essential. Rarely will anyone who is inclined to comforts and bad habits be capable of wandering aimlessly through the city for hours. The pace of the flâneur may be slow or fast, according to his mood and the weather in the city. There are moments in which you can experiment with a slow walk, so as to caress the ground of your most loved road with your foot. People should be considered with detachment if they get annoyed and complain when you are a nuisance for their progress. Even when he walks slowly against the current of the busy, the flâneur will never appear hesitant or, even worse, dull-witted like the simply idle person. There are other moments, however, when the flâneur feels the need to plant his feet firmly on the ground: advancing quickly, his shoulders rolling, his gaze fixed ahead, displaying confidence. People move to one side, intimidated, the road opens before him. In the specific case of contemporary Paris, in order to be able to practice flânerie with full tranquility it would be best to have a physical constitution of some robustness, so as to discourage assaults from delinquents and pick-pockets.

As for the look and style of clothing most appropriate for the flâneur, there could be some controversy over any proposed guidelines. In the past the flâneur was a dandy. In his desire to stand out from the crowds of clerks and workers, he sported a recherché style and expensive clothes. But nothing could be more absurd, today, than to seek to dress better than others in order to stand out from the mass. Especially in Paris, where everyone is a self-elected arbiter of good taste and fashion expert. Thus there are no particular recommendations regarding how the flâneur should dress. In my opinion, the best solution is to appear neither too smart, nor too casual, so as to pass unobserved. The flâneur is fundamentally a lone wolf – complete freedom of movement and autonomy in decision-making are the features that define his operations. Flânerie is therefore an activity to be carried out alone. In some very rare cases one can be a flâneur with a companion: in the company of a person with whom one has developed a profound communion of spirit and with whom one has therefore a feeling that is now close to solitude. Walking in a group, however, can never be considered as flânerie. Expressions such as, *Come for some flânerie with us through the shops of Marais*, or *Sunday: flânerie by bike on the Loire*, used by some travel agencies specialized in "cultured" or élite tourism, are completely absurd.

Flânerie is certainly not an activity that can be engaged in only in Paris. Indeed, the most common error consists of thinking that in order to enjoy a walk in freedom you have to go to a place renowned for tourism, or to some place of particular historical or artistic interest. Of course, the city where the flânerie is engaged in should ideally be large enough, and its structure sufficiently complex and various, so as to allow for full advantage to be taken of the activity. However, I have never come across, and I do not believe such a place exists, an urban area so ordinary or lacking in interest that flânerie is rendered impossible there. What distinguishes the flâneur, the element that elevates him above ordinary people, is indeed the particular relationship that he establishes with the space surrounding him. The very fact of wishing to travel continuously is if anything a symptom of an incapacity to appreciate the richness of details and therefore the splendor of the world. The day in which you decline an invitation to see a film or a concert in order to walk along roads that you already know, the day in which you say no to a journey to some island paradise so as to contemplate the greyness of your own city in the rain… well, that's the day you will know you are a true flâneur.

3.

A day in the life of a flâneur

Rive Gauche

In the 7th arrondissement of Paris, not far from the monumental complex of Les Invalides, there is a church in the eclectic style dedicated to Saint Francis Xavier. It is a late nineteenth-century building, of medium size, not much visited by tourists and not even very well known by Parisians. The church was supposed to close the perspective of a planned boulevard that was never built, leading from the Invalides to the Seine. The Saint-François-Xavier building, though architecturally less impressive and noteworthy than other Parisian churches, houses some interesting relics, works of art and attractions. Among these, the one that more than any other has caught my interest, indeed I might say has fascinated me from the first time I saw it, is Tintoretto's *The Last Supper*, in the sacristy.

It was painted in Venice in 1559 and reached Paris in the Napoleonic era. It is one of the Venetian master's many *Last Suppers*, certainly not the most famous, and yet, for reasons I will soon explain, it is so important to me that I have decided to spend today, my day off, paying it a visit.

It's eight o'clock and I look out of the window. The sky is pale, faded. It has the same color as the façades lined up along the street. The shop shutters are still lowered. A car passes in silence. I relinquish the warmth of my bed, spurred on by the smell of coffee. I prepare to go out to visit the painting by Jacopo Robusti, Tintoretto, a painting that I already know well, but which I like to see again now and then, when I happen to be near the church that houses it. To reach Saint-François-Xavier today I'll have to undertake quite a long walk: across the 5th, the 6th, to reach the 7th arrondissement. It'll take me at least an hour, but it'll be a good opportunity to observe some details of the Left Bank that I usually miss. This plan, going to see Tintoretto's painting, offers me the perfect pretext for a bit of flânerie. Here I am, ready: wearing comfortable clothes, but quite smart. The only clothes appropriate for a city like Paris. On the street people are surly, absorbed by their rushing and their worries, you might even say they're angry. Curiously, the Parisians and the tourists share this state of mind. There's a lot of unease in the air today, there are many things to do. Business to be attended to, clients and salespeople to be satisfied. For the tourists there are many things to see, and a great number of photographs to be taken.

But the flâneur, the connoisseur of Paris, manifests a certain detachment from the goals of earning and of taking advantage of others. He consecrates his day to the study and the cult of the city. The first pleasure one feels in being a flâneur is precisely that of appreciating one's own alterity, one's difference compared to the common people.

It's nine o'clock and I'm walking through the Latin Quarter, a place I've read a hundred novels about, and I know a thousand facets of its history. It's an area rich in memories, in ruins, in institutions. When you walk through the 5th arrondissement you mysteriously enter into contact with times gone by. And yet, to enjoy Paris fully, it's not necessary to remember every historical episode or to learn the list of the kings of France by heart. The relationship that the flâneur establishes with the city and with history is more intimate, direct, almost physical. I pass close by the Hôtel de Cluny. I sniff the old stone to smell the odor of the centuries. With all this walking through the city, I have developed a veneration for the buildings of the past and for ruins. They allow me to perceive time's flow in a tangible way. To the point where I'm almost upset to see in this neighborhood the results of the incessant works of restoration: although they are indispensable for the conservation of the monuments, they tend to classify them in a more abstract and mental dimension. Rue Serpente, Rue Danton, Rue Saint-André des Arts. In the small streets of the area the sidewalks are narrow and one walks briskly. I'm engaged in physical combat with those passing. People walk quickly, each towards their own goal. But I linger to admire the windows of the antique shops, true *Wunderkammer* of the 1600s. I advance slowly, but decidedly westward, towards the parish of Saint-François-Xavier, towards Tintoretto's *Last Supper*.

Francisco de Jasso Azpilcueta Atondo y Aznares de Javier, in French François Xavier, was a Jesuit missionary, canonized in 1622 by Pope Gregory XV. Born in Navarra in 1506 of a noble family, he studied at the Sorbonne and was one of the founders of the Society of Jesus before moving to Italy where he was ordained as a priest in 1537. Francis Xavier was nominated papal nuncio for the Indies and personified the spirit of adventure of many explorers of the 1500s. He carried out his pastoral work in the Portuguese colony of Goa, on the island of Ceylon and in Japan, without ever settling permanently in one place. He learned several languages and had extraordinary encounters with cultures and traditions distant from those of Europe. He converted many and founded several Christian communities. Struck by a violent fever in Canton in China in 1552, he died there at just 46 years of age. Considered an emblem of that burning and combative faith that drives missionaries, many churches throughout the world are dedicated to him, including this one that I am about to visit yet again, commissioned by the Society of Foreign Missions of Paris.

Unlike Francis Xavier, the flâneur doesn't travel to discover ever-new cities and countries. The flâneur knows how to appreciate the infinite variations and the nuances of the places that he already knows. This is why I often find myself becoming attached to areas or urban landscapes most people might find lacking in interest, but which I love walking through and visiting habitually. Not being a missionary, motivation for my peregrinations stems from my love of beauty and of the city. Indeed, I don't think I would be so keen on visiting the church of Saint-François-Xavier if it didn't house Tintoretto's magnificent canvas. Nevertheless, sooner or later something happens that takes the solitary walking man beyond being a simple hedonist and idler. In the labyrinth of the city, the flâneur makes his own destiny. Walking freely without a specific aim is an affirmation of his autonomy in action and in thought. The flâneur moves through Paris as though he were at home, enjoying a spectacle that is always vivid and various, without paying any entrance fee, without being either a client or a consumer. The flâneur in Paris is neither a spectator nor a movie extra: he is the director of the grand film of the city.

It is not yet ten o'clock: having the whole day ahead of me for my flânerie, I decide to lengthen my route slightly and to cross through the Luxembourg Gardens, proceeding in a westerly direction. Grey days like this one offer the ideal moment for admiring the Senate Building through the play of the water of the fountains, an architecture that recalls the splendor of the Italian Renaissance palaces. I sit for a moment on a bench to enjoy the tweeting of the birds in the trees when I see a beautiful young woman with long black hair some thirty meters away, she too sitting on a bench. She has a large book with a grey cover in her hands. She is reading. I look more closely, but I can't make out the title. I would like to be able to ignore her and to continue my dispassionate contemplation of the world around me. But the pure lines of her face, the slim, inviting shapes of her body, the elegant dress, the elevated and literary context of our meeting, these things attract me inexorably and spur me on to meet her. I study the surrounding space with attention and it seems to me she is unaccompanied. I therefore decide to move closer, perhaps under the pretext of asking her what she's reading, or perhaps for some advice on my future readings. It's the perfect moment for a romantic encounter: just the two of us chatting on a bench, on a pale November morning, in the heart of Paris! Driven by enthusiasm I get up and set off towards her, when an old man who is passing by, walking stick in his hand, suddenly deviates from his trajectory and sits right next to the girl, in the only position available. I find myself standing there, motionless just a few steps from the bench. The old man looks at me suspiciously, gripping his stick – perhaps he thinks I'm a pickpocket. And so I prefer to abandon my plan, at least for the moment, and I move away. After all, approaching her in these circumstances would be a bit dodgy. Irritated by this small inconvenience, I decide to wait there for a while, for the old man to get up. So I wander through the Luxembourg Gardens. I observe the pigeons, not so very different from humans in their behavior, busy seeking to satisfy their primary needs. They peck the ground with their beaks seeking invisible particles of food. And they don't hesitate to peck their peers if any of them dare to come close. After having spent a good half hour as a true timewaster, visiting various corners of the park, I find myself covered in dust, from my shoes to the hem of my coat, because of the dry earth of the pathways that are a feature there. On seeing that neither the old man – he now seems to be dozing on his walking stick – nor the young woman, still immersed in her reading, appear to have any intention of getting up and leaving the bench, I decide to abandon the area and continue my walk.

I leave the Luxembourg Gardens behind me and set off towards the church of Saint-François-Xavier to see the beloved painting by Tintoretto. I am aware of the fact that the most famous among the painter's various *Last Suppers* is the one in Venice, in the Basilica di San Giorgio Maggiore. And even other paintings, such as the *Last Supper* in the San Martino cathedral in Lucca, are considered by critics to be of greater artistic value compared to the Parisian work. Perhaps The Last Supper wasn't even Tintoretto's favorite subject, but simply one of the most called for by his clients: thus the painter was forced, every time he was commissioned to work on the theme, to invent a variant and excogitate a different formal solution. In the painting I am about to admire there is a truly surprising feature. Judas, who is about to betray Christ, is depicted in the foreground, his back to us so that the observer can see the bag of coins in his hand. This is the main reason why I love the Parisian version of the Supper: not so much for the inclined position of the table, nor because of the gloomy atmosphere that is a forerunner of the scenes of Baroque painting, but above all because of the terrible emotion that the painting conveys, rendering the observer involved and complicit in the betrayal of Christ. I also appreciate the solution adopted in the perspective, which ties together the characters depicted, in particular the accentuated contrast between the agitation of some of the apostles, busy in a heated discussion, and the seraphic calm of Christ. Of course, you can view this painting in an art catalogue, even on the Internet, but it is only a real-life and close encounter, in the right light, that allows you to savor Tintoretto's fine stylistic nuances, to recognize the artist's lines and his brushwork.

And so I head towards the church. I find myself on Boulevard Saint-Germain, on the western boundary of the 5th arrondissement. I take a little detour to observe the beautiful people sitting at the café tables, to breathe the typical atmosphere of this corner of Paris. Rue Grégoire de Tours, Rue des Quatre Vents. Then there are some small streets, near the Mabillon metro station, which are very busy by night, but now peaceful. Passing in front of the pubs I can breathe the smell of the wood steeped in beer. Now I am in Rue de Rennes and then I turn right, passing in front of the church of Saint-Germain-des-Prés. At the Café de Flore sit the famous people, the *starlettes* of the cinema, the show-business acrobats, the footballers and the fashion celebrities. They drink their coffees motionless, sitting in the windows, there to watch the others or to be watched. The flâneur instead takes joy in his own anonymity. Only when you pass by unobserved along the streets of Paris can you enjoy complete freedom and breathe the essence of the possible in the air. I now pass through the small streets adjacent to the square, looking at the sweet shops, the furniture and the chic clothes boutiques. The women linger before the windows, dressed in furs, loaded with bags and more bags, accompanied by distinguished-looking men. Rue Jacob, Rue Bonaparte, Rue de Seine. The houses here are low, tiny. The streets are narrow. You might say it's like being in a provincial city. And yet the details in the façades, on the doors, on the balconies, manifest all the signs of a sophisticated elegance. It's certainly not the impressiveness or the grandiloquence of the buildings themselves that tells you you're in Paris – it is the sheer style. All the elements of the urban landscape combine together into an extraordinary whole. It is absurd to think of those who, despite living here, miss no opportunity – not even on the shortest of vacations – to take themselves off to far off cities and countries, when the spectacle offered by just one of the arrondissements, let alone the entire metropolis, would be enough to satisfy the most avid flâneur! Paris is like oxygen to a dying man, a dose of opium that comforts those addicted to urban beauty. There is no great despair that cannot be alleviated by the spectacle of Paris. There is no misadventure that cannot be forgotten, at least momentarily, thanks to its magnificence. Nevertheless, this city concedes itself neither to the busy man, nor to the tourist. Paris belongs only to those who are not in a rush, to those who abandon the logic of production and consumption, managing to free themselves at least for an instant from the general race towards profit and taking advantage of others.

On finally reaching the level of Rue du Bac, now no more than five hundred meters separate me from my longed-for painting. But before being able to admire the masterpiece, it would be a good idea to keep my strength up by eating a little something. It's almost one o'clock and I haven't had anything for hours. The most natural solution would be to sit at a table in a good restaurant and order a real meal. The restaurants all have little blackboards outside with lists of their dishes: vegetable quiche, duck or goose foie gras, game or fish pate on bread, leek soup, onion soup gratinée, roast chicken with french fries, fruits of the sea, rare duck, sole à la meunière, steak with tartar sauce, cheese selections... But on reflection, the idea of sitting at a table to stuff oneself might be somehow blasphemous or paradoxical for a person who's heading, almost on a pilgrimage, to stand before *The Last Supper*. Further to this, knowing the most certainly non-proverbial rapidity of French waiters and cooks, I'd end up wasting too much time. Better then to have a more frugal meal. The flâneur avoids luxury and manages to appreciate even the simplicity of an improvised lunch. I could stroll towards Saint-Michel and have one of those famous "Greek sandwiches" with fatty meat, onions, mayonnaise and salad. Or a Nutella crêpe, typical boulevard food. But these two dishes appear to me to be no less inappropriate for an athlete of the city stroll, which is what a flâneur should be. On further reflection regarding the pros and cons of the various possibilities the city offers, I decide in the end to head down Rue du Bac and to go to the Bon Marché to try a few of their famous *macarons*. Like colored communion wafers, *macarons* are an almost intangible and spiritual nutrition: they provide a good quantity of sugar and don't represent a challenge for one's digestive system. And then, while I'm heading down Rue du Bac southwards, something pleasantly unexpected presents itself: in a "workshop" along the street there's a vernissage taking place. Paris is famous for its inaugurations of art exhibitions and this neighborhood is full of them. Usually, for such events, the galleries offer a free snack. This is why, together with the bargain hunters and aspiring art critics, these events always attract a numerous group of punters, curiosity-seekers and scroungers.

Thanks to my smart clothes I have no difficulty in getting into the gallery. Those present ignore me completely and I move discreetly towards the table laid out for the buffet and I begin my feast. First course: Greek salad and fresh orange juice. The others move towards the work of art the exhibition is dedicated to and which occupies the center of the space. A woman, whose tone of voice suggests she's part way between an art expert and a saleswoman, begins speaking:

> Ladies and gentlemen, thank you for being here and welcome to the Seven Seas Gallery. Today it is my pleasure to present a much discussed and much acclaimed work of art, on which rivers of ink have been expended and which has been the subject of many

lectures in the best universities. I am truly moved to be able to present it to you here after its long journey, give that it comes to us direct from New York. It is, of course, a work by the Anonymous Afro-American, the celebrated art installation titled *Mother Africa*.

Out of curiosity, while I eat my salad, I move closer to the group of observers to get a better look at the work on the gallery floor. The installation consists of a tin bucket filled with sand into which a stick has been placed. The art expert continues her declamation. I observe the reactions of her audience. There are some emblematic faces, so representative of the Parisian intellectual caste. Men with slightly feminine features and with thin faces. Women with short hair who exude an air of severity and gravity.

Second course: caviar crouton and a glass of Chablis.

> … observe now the sapient dialogue between the grains of sand and the solidity of the wood: a dialectic between soft and hard materials that clearly bears the mark of Surrealism. And observe the artificially spontaneous way in which the stick is plunged into the sand. Note how the presence of the pole in this context evokes above all the absence of the hand …

Third course: salami sandwich with butter and cucumber accompanied by a glass of Saint-Émilion.

> … thus we reach the most profound of meanings, the philosophical essence of this masterpiece. This work indeed offers us a representation of remoteness, of the things-that-will-soon-no-longer-be …

Fourth course and grand finale: chocolate mousse with a glass of champagne.

> Analyzing the chromatic play, ultimately we can note how the refined Cassel earth pigment of the wood expresses here the night of humanity, the crisis in bourgeois values. What the artist brings splendidly to the scene here and what you see before you today are thus the aporias and the contradictions of modern society ...

Sated with food and with words, I leave the art gallery. I now feel in good shape, well nourished and rested, ready for my meeting with Tintoretto's masterpiece. After all, right now – it's three in the afternoon – is the perfect time for appreciating the painting: indeed a more delicate sun will now caress it, penetrating diagonally from the sacristy windows. This dimmer light would seem to me to be ideal for a work that, although aiming at a certain scenographic and spectacular effect typical of its painter, seeks at the same time to establish a relationship of complicity with the observer. As it sends its rays at just the right inclination, the sun appears to stroke the surface of the painting, rendering even more dramatic the strength of the chiaroscuro that marks Tintoretto's energetic style. A scenic tension that you can only perceive properly if you visit the painting in person.

I am now impatient to reach the church, my stride now becomes more decided. I proceed towards the 7th arrondissement, along the interminable Boulevard

Saint-Germain. Here the cafés become rarer, while the high-fashion and luxury furniture shops multiply. But just when I am about to cross the boundary of the 7th arrondissement, I spot the beautiful girl I'd seen in the Luxembourg Gardens on the other side of the boulevard. She, too, is walking rapidly, but in the opposite direction. I am again attracted by her slender figure, by her long black hair, by the womanliness she exudes with every step. The fact I should see her right here, twice in the same day and at a distance of just a few hours, could be a sign of destiny. Or perhaps it's just a simple coincidence. Whatever, I have no time to waste: the best thing, in these cases, is a direct approach on the street. I am decided to speak to her frankly, without shyness or hesitation. It's usually very busy, but I have no trouble crossing the boulevard, which now is strangely free of traffic. Unfortunately, however, just as I am about to reach her, a uniformed policeman stops me.

"Halt!"

"Sorry, but what's going on?" I ask, astonished.

"Haven't you heard? There's an anti-government student demonstration taking place. Please wait here while the march passes by. It'll just be a few minutes."

The crowd is very thick: around the group of students who advance with the big banner and which forms, so to speak, the head of the line, some curiosity-seekers and even some tourists have joined in. Towards the end there's the usual rear guard of funsters and hangers-on. One of these guys comes up to me singing some old song and offers me some wine.

"My friend, how are you today?"

"I'm fine, thanks."

"Come on, have a sip of some Bordeaux! A good day to you!"

"Thanks, and you too!"

While the march passes before me, I try to keep track of the shape of the girl moving away towards the east, along Boulevard Saint-Germain. Her figure becomes ever smaller, just like a star vanishing on the horizon. She's just a little pinpoint by now. As soon as the march has passed, the police signal that we can start moving again. So I set off running towards her. I have to push my way through the crowd. After a few minutes, near the Odéon station, I think I see her shape: there she is, two hundred meters ahead of me. I'm determined to reach her and to speak to her. She crosses Boulevard Saint-Michel almost running and heads toward the Sorbonne. She seems to be in a hurry. But when I'm just one hundred meters from her, she turns to the left and enters a building. If the distance isn't playing tricks on me, it's a cinema. I get closer and see that indeed it is: one of those old cinemas that are a feature of this area. They're showing a classic Italian film, *Il grido*, by Antonioni. With no delay I enter and pay for a ticket at the box office. I hope I'll manage to find her. As we all know, the cinema is the ideal place for a real encounter, for a complicit game of gazes and, eventually, if there's any chance of sitting next to her, for a more daring flirt.

"The film's already started, hurry up!" says the

ticket girl.

As soon as I enter the darkness I notice with surprise that even though it's just an ordinary November afternoon, there are a lot of film-goers. I stand for a while trying to identify the girl with the black hair among the rows of lined-up heads.

"Sit down, please," says a man wearing glasses.

"That's enough now, just sit still," adds another.

I have to take a seat and wait patiently for the end of the film. Undoubtedly it's a work of considerable artistic and cultural interest. And yet, when you're a flâneur, you inevitably have your senses and your imagination so satisfied, so overloaded by the sight of the spectacle of the city that a film, no matter how poetically elevated, risks losing its interest. How could a flâneur, in love with Paris, the harbinger of freedom, ever find pleasure in locking himself away in a dark room, resigned to witnessing the projection of a film on a wall?

And so I fall asleep. And I dream. I am in the Luxembourg Gardens, the girl with the black hair is sitting on the bench and is reading a book. It's a large book with a grey cover. My shoes and my coat are covered in dust, but I pluck up my courage and I move towards her. The girl looks up and smiles complicitly. She gestures to me to keep quiet and to sit next to her. She hands me the book. It is the collected letters of Francis Xavier. Suddenly an old man appears, threatening in appearance. He walks towards us quickly, brandishing a stick. The girl gets up and runs away, leaving me alone and shocked on the bench. "See you in church," she shouts as she runs, "in front of Tintoretto's painting." At that point the lights come on and I wake up. The film has finished. I'm ready to leap up and start looking for the girl, but unfortunately no one moves. Like all self-respecting film-buffs, this Parisian audience wants to read carefully the credits, to the very last line. Then, finally, the film soundtrack is suddenly interrupted and everyone stands up. I start looking for the girl. There are many women. They are putting on hats and wrapping voluminous scarves around their necks. None of them have long black hair like hers. I try to push my way towards the exit.

"What on earth … where are your manners!?"

"How rude! Pushing through like that … "

Finally I find myself back on the street, Rue de la Sorbonne. Unfortunately, no matter how carefully I scrutinize both sides, there's no trace of my girl. I'm disappointed to have lost her again, for the second time on the same day. "In big cities, a person lost is lost forever," I repeat to myself with sadness. But then I look around and I think that, in the end, Paris isn't a big city: it's just a big village. And sooner or later I'll probably rediscover her.

It's now six o'clock in the evening. The sun is setting, but why not see Tintoretto's *Last Supper* even at dusk, in the light of the sacristy lamps? The painting will appear even gloomier, almost foretelling the dark atmospheres of the 1600s and presaging the freakishness of the Baroque. Now I'm going along Boulevard Saint-Germain for the second time in a westerly direction. I try to walk more quickly, without letting myself be distracted by the details of the urban landscape. I walk absorbed, savoring the poetic melancholic vein that is so typical of Paris. I observe the general sense of splendor and decline: the old glorious buildings are occupied and corrupted by the ephemeral glitter of the luxury shops. I observe how a basic sadness is accompanied, in the passers-by, with a certain inhibition, with a certain solemnity. My stride is rapid, imperative. It is in tune with the symphony of the city. Even the fatigue that comes over me after a full day's walking floods me with a sort of ascetic detachment: it puts a certain distance between me and the pettiness of the quotidian. Even the world of the Spectacle and of consumption in my eyes loses all importance, and finally I reach a more profound and synthetic vision of Paris.

Rue Saint-Dominique, Rue de Bourgogne. I should head straight on southwards to reach the longed-for church, but when I reach the golden dome of Les Invalides I decide to lengthen my route slightly to admire the grand Esplanade on the north front. I want to breathe the fresh and humid air of the river. The church of Saint-François-Xavier is now nearby, getting there is a matter of minutes. I take Rue de Grenelle and come to the imposing building of Les Invalides. I stop on the grass. I take a deep breath. This is an important moment, which allows me to regain my concentration. After having dealt with all the obstacles along the way, I can finally focus my soul on the only real reason, on the supreme aim of my day: Tintoretto's *Last Supper*. But just when I've decided to leave the lawn, I meet a middle-aged couple who have been picnicking on the grass. It seems there's a celebration. They turn to me:

"Excuse us, Monsieur? Monsieur, please come here!" shouts the man.

I glance at them, pretending not to hear. What do they want from me?

"Yes, you … come here!" the woman chirps up.

Fearing I may be considered rude, I walk over to them.

"Bon soir! Listen, my wife and I were married exactly thirty years ago. We've come back here, where we had one of our wedding photographs taken, so that we could have our portrait done again in the same position at sunset, thirty years on! Don't you think that's a great idea? We were going to take a selfie, but on seeing you pass by I thought we might ask you to be our photographer."

What a pain! The man perceives my hesitation and adds, "Don't worry, I've brought all the necessary gear." He proceeds to extract from his bag a large camera and holds it out to me.

"Here you go, first rate equipment. A very expensive brand. Japanese."

It's too late now to refuse him the favor. After all, the church really is just round the corner, I can almost feel its presence.

"Listen, stand over there, please … You see that white chalk mark I made on the path? Just take two steps back, thanks."

"Fine, that's exactly where the photographer was thirty years ago!" exclaims his wife radiantly.

The pair of them put on a pose and I take the photograph. "That's it," I say, returning the camera.

"But no, hang on," says the husband, "the exposure wasn't long enough, it's almost night. I want another one. But remember to keep still. Don't move while you're taking it."

So I return to the mark and take more photographs.

"Listen, no ... perhaps I didn't explain very well," says the man. "The dome has to be in the very center of the image. And try not to cut my wife's feet off, please!"

After a few more attempts, I finally manage to fulfill all their requirements.

"I'd say that's fine, we'll post it on our social networks. Just a minute, though ... Listen, for our anniversary my wife would like to go and get changed, put on her wedding dress and take another photo. Just like thirty years ago. It'll only take a few minutes, you'll see. In the meantime I could treat you to a slice of cake and a drink."

Horrified at the prospect of another wait, and in the company of this pushy man to boot, I invent an excuse. I declare myself sorry not to be able to help and take my leave. I head down Boulevard des Invalides and in a few minutes I'm in Place du Président Mithouard. Here I am, finally, before the blessed church, the slightly run-down, but reassuring building of Saint-François-Xavier. The outline is symmetrical and square, lacking in verticality. The façade is clearly inspired by the Italian Renaissance. The bas-relief on the pediment represents a familiar figure: Francis Xavier baptizing the peoples of India and Japan. I move closer slowly, I want to savor this triumphal entrance.

To tell the truth, I'm tired. I've had a rather busy day, but it is right now, after hours and hours of fatigue, that one attains a state of ataraxy, that imperturbability of the senses that best favors an approach to a work of art as complex as Tintoretto's. Before observing a painting of such artistic significance, and of even greater religious meaning, one has to be well prepared: it is fundamental to be not only in adequate physical condition, but in the best spiritual state too. Getting off a tourist bus early in the morning, with your legs stiff and your brain not working, your companions yawning – that's not the way to appreciate the profound mystery of *The Last Supper*. Thus I ascend the steps that lead to the entrance with a certain solemnity, holding my breath. With some self-importance I adjust the lapels and collar of my jacket and my trousers. Then I extend my arm, I take hold of the handle and push the large, dark wood door. But it fails to move. It's locked. I wonder, astonished, what has happened. So I knock, but no one responds. I wait a moment and try again. After a few minutes I think I hear some steps inside the church. A slight noise that becomes gradually louder. Then the bolt moves and the door creaks as it opens. Out of the darkness appears the Caravaggio-like face of an elderly woman.

"Monsieur, the church is closed," she says in a curt tone.

"Good evening, I've come to see a painting

that's in the sacristy: could I come in just for a minute or two?"

"It's half past eight, we are not open at this time."

"But how can that be, excuse me ... aren't you open until nine in the evening? I read the times on your website."

"Ah! No, Monsieur," the old woman replies, "I think you refer to the summer timetable. In October we adopt our winter timetable, so we close at eight o'clock. The church closed half an hour ago."

"In that case, please allow me to apologize, Madame, for having bothered you at this time," I say, emphasizing an expression of grief on my face. Then I add, "Despite this, my sincere passion for art and my devotion to François Xavier give me the courage to ask of you a personal favor. If I beg you to let me in at this hour it is certainly not to satisfy any vain curiosity, nor to take a few photographs. As you well know, this church houses Tintoretto's *The Last Supper*, a seminal work of art, and I have walked all day to reach it."

"I have already told you that it's not possible, I am not authorized to let you in at this time. Please, don't insist!"

"Madame, look closely at my tired face, my dust-covered shoes and overcoat: do you have any idea of the difficulties I have had to face, how many unrecountable vicissitudes have overtaken me today, before finally being able to reach this church, like a poor pilgrim before your door?"

"Listen to me well ... if you really want to see

that painting you can come back here tomorrow. The church opens to the public at eight o'clock in the morning. Thank you and good night."

Thus having spoke, the old woman takes a step backwards and her face gradually disappears into the darkness. I try to sneak a look inside the church. But it's too dark: you can only just make out the three naves and down at the bottom, near the altar, a few flickering candles. Then on the right, I think I can make out a glow that corresponds, but I can't be sure, to the entrance of the sacristy. The big door closes slowly, accompanied by the loud creaking. Once again, the bolt moves. Then the ever-slighter steps of the old woman moving away.

4.

Once there was the flâneur

> *The flâneur can be born anywhere;*
> *he can live only in Paris.*
>
> (An anonymous flâneur)

In nineteenth-century Paris there were some men known as "flâneurs". They used to walk alone along the Seine, in front of the major stations and through the *passages couverts*. They used to chat up the beautiful girls, observe the scenery, the shop windows or antique prints and they even, apparently, took a turtle for a walk on a leash. The origin of the French word *flâneur* is uncertain. According to *Le Grand Robert de la langue française* the term flâneur derives from the Norman verb "flanner" ("to laze", "to waste time"), documented as early as 1638, but certainly older than that and, according to the *Trésor de la langue française*, probably derived from the ancient Scandinavian "flana" ("to run here and there"). The *Grand Dictionnaire universel du XIX siècle*, by Pierre Larousse – a positivist-inspired work — argues that the term flâneur derives instead from the Irish "flanni", meaning "libertine". The first examples in any case date from the early 1800s: the word spread progressively in France from the 1830s onwards.

Despite the ambiguous etymology of the word *flâneur*, from the descriptions in literary writings and in vignettes from that time we have a quite clear outline of the character: it is the portrait of a new man, the product of modern European society, and of a new urban style of life. The flâneur is not the walker-philosopher — who we can find literary models for as far back as ancient times and, more recently, in the *Promenades solitaires* of Jean-Jacques Rousseau — the walker-philosopher who searches natural environments for spurs to meditation and deeper spiritual insight. Instead he is bourgeois, a dandy with remarkable critical intelligence and driven by an insatiable curiosity for the varied and ever-changing spectacle of the modern city. The renewal of Paris, in particular the opening of the *passages couverts* and, later, the radical modernization established by the prefect Haussmann, transformed public space into an "interior" space that the masses could furnish and inhabit. Modern Paris is landscape and interior, the Promised Land for vagabonds and flâneurs. In the free space of the post-revolutionary capital, the flâneur clearly stood out from the crowd, due both to the higher social status that enabled him to "waste his time" and to his capacity for interpreting the landscape of the city, which had become, in his eyes, an enigma to be deciphered. The prevailing interest in the world of phenomena and the flâneur's freedom of movement contrasted on the one hand with the principles of the metaphysical and religious tradition on which pre-industrial civilization was based and, on the other, with the dogma of productivity which held sway over the nascent bourgeois society. Hence the paradoxical nature of the flâneur, the shattered mirror of modernity. He acts out his own dissonant idleness right in the beating heart of the city and he steeps himself in the tumult of the crowd while seeking to maintain a critical detachment.

The flâneur appears in the first half of the nineteenth century in a corpus of texts of various kinds – later defined by Walter Benjamin as "panoramic literature" – which includes serialized novels, pamphlets and travel guides. The very first description of our character is contained in an anonymous pamphlet of 1806, published in Paris: *Le Flâneur au salon ou M. Bon-Homme: examen joyeux des tableaux, mêlé de vaudevilles*. In this little book of not quite 32 pages, Monsieur Bon-Homme recounts his walk, to tell the truth a somewhat conformist one, through the main attractions of the French capital. The brief narration concludes with the traditional visit to the Louvre and with the description of some paintings exhibited there. Two years later, in 1808, we find the verb *flâner* in the *Dictionnaire du bas langage* by Hautel, with this definition: "to wander purposelessly from one place to another; to do nothing; to live an errant and vagabond life". The word flâneur also spread quickly through the tourist guidebooks and travel writing that had Paris as their topic. One example is the 1826 recount written by Jean-Baptiste Auguste Aldéguier: *Le flâneur, ou mon voyage à Paris, mes aventures dans cette capitale, et détails exacts de ce que j'y ai remarqué de curieux, et de nécessaire à connaître.*

In the wake of this tradition, Balzac introduces the flâneur as a literary character in *Physiologie du mariage* in 1829 and subsequently uses him again in other novels of the *Comédie Humaine*. Flânerie is described by Balzac as a science, an urban epistemology in every sense, a method of work and research that is in strict correlation with novel writing. Perhaps the point of maximum originality in the "panoramic" tradition is attained in the 1837 novella *Facino Cane*, in which Balzac describes a most singular character: a man who in order to recover from the exhausting study that absorbs him during the day, sets out on nocturnal walks in a state of deep interior excitement. This acute observer spies on and follows passers-by along the streets of Paris, filling his own interior void with their stories. Facino Cane thus anticipates the figure of the detective or urban investigator, typical of crime novels.

From the 1830s onwards the flâneur became a popular figure in Paris. In 1831, an "anonymous flâneur" signed the article *Le flâneur à Paris* collected in the volume, *Paris, ou le livre de cent-et-un*. With this article the flâneur is instated officially as one of the representative characters of the French capital and of the modernity that it symbolizes. Among the *Physiologies* published by Aubert in the years 1840–1860, we find the *Physiologie du flâneur* of 1841, written by Louis Huart and complemented with vignettes by

Daumier and Maurisset. The *Physiologies*, inspired by the physiognomic studies of Lavater, offer an accurate, albeit satirical representation of the social figures of nineteenth-century Paris. They appeared as inserts to newspapers and were enormously successful and much read. And the *feuilletons* dedicated to the flâneur certainly contributed to increasing the popularity of the term, introducing into the collective imaginary this human type. In the satirical tone that is a feature of the *Physiologies*, Huart distinguishes the flâneur from other types of people who did not have the necessary qualities to be identified with this name. For example, the old codgers who, after their daily walk of "twenty-five steps", sit on a bench and chat until dinnertime are not flâneurs. Those who walk their dog are not flâneurs, and neither are those of the bourgeoisie who on Sunday evening walk up and down the boulevards with their families. The flâneur is clearly distinguishable from the *musard*, the layabout who takes up to three hours to cover the small distance between the Saint-Denis and the Saint-Martin gates. Lacking in intelligence and critical spirit, the *musard* proceeds slowly, stupidly attracted by the shop windows, by the street jugglers, dragged along passively by the crowd. The *badaud étranger* instead, the tourist visiting Paris, has the rapid stride and the acute eye of the flâneur, but his movements are determined by a strict timetable, a precise program. Then there is the *batteur de pavé*, the poor man of no fixed abode, who although being an expert connoisseur of the city, is lacking in that elegance and the refined aesthetic taste that characterizes the true flâneur. The Daumier and Maurissat vignettes that illustrate the text of the *Physiologie* depict the flâneur as a fully blown bourgeois, dressed in impeccable clothes and in a relaxed and tranquil pose. The flâneur knows the fashions and the manners of fine Parisian society: he is distinguished in his eccentric elegance and walks carrying his walking stick in his pocket, in line with a fashion of the epoch. Unlike his fellow citizens who are perpetually harried by the chores of daily life, the flâneur roams where his fancy takes him, "right or left, without rhyme or reason". Flânerie is thus a sign of critical intelligence and moral stature, an exercise in freedom that can ennoble the spirit. A man lifts himself above other living beings only when he knows how to be a flâneur, carrying out a voluntary action without a purpose, an act of emancipation with regard to the ties of nature and of society.

The definitive literary consecration of the flâneur came only two decades later with Charles Baudelaire: a central element of his poetry, as expressed in the *Tableaux parisiens*, is in fact the metaphor of the city as text, with reference to the role of the walking man as a reader and interpreter of the urban scene. In his collection of essays, *Le Peintre de la vie moderne* (1863), Baudelaire credits artistic modernity with the special quality of seeking and fixing the new form of beauty that ties the ephemeral to that which is eternal. He emphasizes the need, therefore, for a renewed aesthetic practice and identifies the caricaturist Costantin Guy as emblematic: an artist capable of plunging into the crowd and roaming the city in search of a revelation to re-depict in his works of art. The connection between flânerie and artistic creation generates furthermore new forms of expression that adapt to the fragmentary nature of experience afforded by urban life and the flashes of insight that bedazzle the walking man.

It is in this very work that we find reference to Poe's 1840 story, "The Man of the Crowd", first translated into French by Baudelaire himself. In this text the American author introduces two characters that, in my opinion, are essential to an understanding of the role of the flâneur in modern culture: a man who observes and analyses the physiognomy of the people in the city crowds and another who goes through the city with no apparent motive, so as to remain surrounded by the multitude. The first character, endowed with exceptional powers of observation and reasoning, strives to interpret the enigmatic landscape of the nineteenth-century metropolis. The second, however, is an odd individual, devoid of identity, who wanders in search of something that the narrator himself, even after prolonged investigation, is unable to determine. This story – using the device of a "double" so typical of Poe – stages the essential duality at the origin of the modern practice of flânerie. On one hand we have the drive, embodied in the character of the detective, to observe and know phenomenal reality: this dynamic follows, in the references to the physiognomy and other empirical sciences, the development of positivist thinking characterizing mid-nineteenth century Europe. On the other hand is the drive, personified by the "man of the crowd" to search for a form of diversion in the external world, rendering the city panorama an escape route from a problematic inner dimension.

The character described by Baudelaire in *Le Peintre de la vie moderne* is afflicted by the same *horror vacui* that plagues Poe's man of the crowd: a typically modern emotion, arising from the disorientation that assails an individual when deprived of the value system that was characteristic of pre-industrial society. Like the detective, Baudelaire's flâneur investigates the truth through careful observation of the world of phenomena, but this operation that he undertakes on city terrain proves antithetical and specular to introspection. The flâneur cannot stand still, having to escape the specter of loneliness and his inner being: he is an individual destined to a perpetual but unfulfilled quest for the meaning of this very act of moving. Actually referring to Poe's story, Baudelaire assigns the flâneur a new and disturbing aspect that was missing from the French tradition of panoramic literature. Baudelaire's artist-flâneur, "a self insatiable of the non-self" (Baudelaire 2003a, p. 692) who reappears in the prose poems of *Spleen de Paris* (1869), remains an ambiguous figure, torn between the desire to stand out from the crowd and a conflicting desire to throw himself into it and lose himself there. A yearning for a diversion from and an eclipsing of one's own identity that may be a consequence of the nihilism and existential disorientation that define modern man.

Starting with the "archetype" established by Baudelaire, reference to the figure of the flâneur would remain alive in France, even in remote artistic forms and experiences, from the realist novel to the twentieth-century avant-garde, and would subsequently gain ground in other European cultures. Limiting ourselves solely to the Parisian setting, the flâneur, a human type with such profoundly characterizing features, can be recognized in the paintings of the Impressionists, who were after all supported by Baudelaire the art critic: these painters, as is known, introduced a new form of perception of space, new urban subjects and an innovative technique with which the vital and ephemeral beauty of modernity could be represented.

Reference to flânerie in the avant-garde movements of the early twentieth century underlines a new way of making use of the city's spaces. The Surrealist authors, active in Paris around the 1920s, made of freedom of movement and the principle of randomness an artistic activity and a method of working. They experimented with new ways for fathoming the poetic potential of walking in the city. The technique of "automatism", in which free rein is given to the unconscious, was applied to the practice of walking the streets, which had to take place with no pre-established destination. Walking aimlessly is an activity that disengages from the stifling imperative of "productivism" and enables perceptions of reality to be overturned and renewed, in an attempt to reconcile daily life with the individual's unconscious impulses and desires. Sustained by literary stereotypes from the nineteenth-century tradition, the Surrealist flâneur, in an almost frantic search for a breakdown in order, or in pursuit of a chimerical female alter ego – like Breton in *Nadja* (1928) or Soupault in *Les Dernières Nuits de Paris* (1928) – is condemned to permanent dissatisfaction, to perennial lack of fulfillment, which is the essential prerequisite for living in the dimension of eternal possibility. Flânerie thus became a *modus vivendi*, a style of life linked to the idea that the drift of the city is an instrument for the discovery of one's self. The distinctive elements of Baudelaire's flâneur were still recognizable: the aimless walking man escapes the "black hole" of consciousness and sustains his crisis-struck individuality through symbolic appropriation of phenomenal reality and in particular the city, symbol of a modern and unfamiliar form of beauty. The flâneur transfigures his own inner self in a symmetrical movement within the metropolitan landscape, lived as an image and transposition of himself. And it was precisely his reading of the Surrealist authors that guided Benjamin in his study of nineteenth-century Parisian society, in which the flâneur rises to become symbol of a cultural and anthropological transformation that seems, in respects that I will seek to illustrate below, to determine the fate of modern man.

5.

Getting lost

Opéra, Rue Saint-Denis

He got up suddenly, in the middle of a sleepless night. He dressed and went down into the street without his wallet, without his phone. Buttoned up in his black overcoat, Bruno walked through the old neighborhood. Paris was not completely silent, but calmer and more composed that usual. The North wind skimmed the pavements, sending litter and empty cans scurrying at the sides of the street. Thus the air was cold and clear and the signs of the closed cafés, sex shops and chemists were visible from far away. Then the line of taxis leading to the Gare de l'Est.

There were nights in which Bruno couldn't sleep. Sometimes sleepiness came on him during the daytime, in front of his computer, at the supermarket or during a conversation. Then, at dusk, his whole being was reawakened and he seemed to grasp something, to gain a profound insight coupled with a bodily frenzy, an excitement he could not contain. For this reason he went out into the street. And that night more than usual he was overcome by a thirst for fullness, for totality. From the moment in which his rising parabola had been suddenly interrupted, in which his future appeared to him like blurred image – the city, for him, had become a mysterious morass, a jumble of passions to be unraveled. The city was an encrypted text, a manuscript he had to decipher. And this was the perfect season, when the trees were skeletal, the smells had faded and delicate silhouettes of things were left on the street like unresolved enigmas. In the dead of night Paris became an abstract city, a mental landscape like a metaphysical painting. In the midst of that strange quietness, he could not remain still. Sleeping or simply relaxing was not possible. So Bruno walked that night towards the Opéra, dressed completely in black.

Along the arc of the boulevards there were still some financial workers, some bank clerks returning home after an evening at the office. With their heads bowed and their ties wrapped round their necks, they walked to the rhythm of a military march, brandishing their closed umbrellas like the pole of some war standard. In those haughty faces marked by worry, in those sharp eyes in their dark circles, Bruno recognized the nightmares of his past and was horrified by them. But that evening the clerks who filed one by one before the fierce lights of the Rex cinema now seemed to be thin and insubstantial figures, almost ethereal. Even the buildings of Boulevard Montmartre seemed to have lost their usual rigor. It is precisely when one walks alone and aimlessly through the city that the certainties and the dogmas of common thought suddenly reveal all their insubstantiality, their partiality. Thus, after years of forced conformism and abnegation, Bruno that evening rediscovered the vital thrill of freedom. He had finally found his vocation: getting lost.

He walked along Boulevard Haussmann. He observed, in the night, the rigorous succession of the architraves, the columns and the pediments. The wrought-iron balconies, black and flowerless, at the second and the fifth floors. The Opéra Garnier bore impassable and grave forms, made even more somber by the nocturnal darkness. Bruno's gaze floated in the tide of white stone. He immersed himself among the stuccoes as they were touched by the car headlamps, shining up there, drunk with light. What excited his imagination were the arcane and nude decorations of the old pediments. The doors, paint flaking like dry lips. In ecstasy, huddled in his overcoat like a second skin, he brushed past the walls of those glorious monuments. He felt as though he'd been condemned to a restless flight, a forward rush. His energy came from an inner Big Bang that had unhinged the repetitive order of past life and had led him in a new direction. His new route was plotted, already decided. His destiny was marked on the façades of the buildings. Along the perimeter of these constructions he recognized his dilemma, he was entering the vicious circle of his torments.

It was deep into the night. Along the streets there was almost no one. Only the homeless and the tramps remained – confused atoms, alone, drifting along the boulevards of the Right Bank. Their silence transformed the landscape of the city into an intimate space, a salon of grotesque masks and the most bizarre disguises. Some occupied a permanent space, making the sidewalk their home. They had built meticulously a shack of cardboard boxes. Others sat on a street corner, next to a cart or suitcase, as if they were about to set off on a journey. They spent their days constantly drunk. Others again were afflicted with a relentless restlessness. They wandered alone through the city, trudging from street to street like tormented souls. They looked for coins in ruts in the tarmac or in gutters at the stations. In the evening they remained motionless on the sidewalk, oblivious, cataleptic, as though paralyzed by stupor. Or else they fell asleep in the most incongruous of poses and in the unlikeliest of places: entrenched in niches along the walls, wrapped in old newspapers like mummies, moribund, in front of bank offices, outside airline headquarters. Sometimes you could see a stream of urine trickling away from their trousers, crossing the sidewalk, forming incomprehensible doodles and running into a storm drain.

Bruno, too, in a certain sense, was a man of no fixed abode. He was unable to bear the silent stasis of a room during the hours of night. He couldn't bear the sight of the white ceiling when he was stretched out on the bed. But what was he doing all alone in the street in the middle of the night? Where was he going? Why had he decided in this way, suddenly, to no longer work, to leave his job and dedicate his life to this drifting with no destination? Well ... this was not easy to explain. Perhaps he had realized that all the aspirations of ordinary people – that long quiet river of the middle class – was not for him. That sort of suicide that he had long fantasized about – a life consisting of small economic ambitions, of familiar comforts, and then a fulltime job that suffocated consciousness – would have sentenced him to a permanent divergence from his true nature, from his deepest desires. Was it perhaps from himself, and from his own psyche that he was fleeing? From the dead end of logic, of introspection? Because Bruno was unable to inhabit the hovel of his ego, an inhospitable and empty place. He preferred to wander through the city, to vanish. May his head be stunned by the cold and the neon lights, like a drifting boat. Outside, at least, there was a hypnotic buzz – the spectacle of the city that offers itself without promises, without meaning; a spectacle which distracts and occupies the restless mind, otherwise prisoner of its painful contradictions.

In truth he felt like a passenger, a spectator of his own motion. Now it was his legs that drove him forward, like a train engine out of control. The more he walked, the more he immersed himself in that sort of orgiastic pleasure that tiredness can bring and the prospect of going back home became unbearable. More and more distinctly he heard a music that rang through the air of the city. And his steps were in tune with this melody. He saw the groups of youngsters who waited, queuing to enter the bars on the street. Time was when he too had been led to seek this form of amusement. Time was when he too had brought his days to the same end, under those cloudy skies, in bars very similar to these. But not now. Now he sought to experience a different emotion, a more profound communion with things. He had embraced the destiny of his city, Paris, which now seemed to adhere to him, to his skin. So, after he had completed his third lap of the entire arc of the boulevards, he suddenly took Rue Saint-Denis and headed south.

Dirt, thought Bruno, was an essential feature of the Parisian atmosphere and landscape. Precisely in this much degraded area of the city this characteristic was becoming more evident, to the point that the walking man was overcome, in the dead of night, by a strange sensation of nihilism and impunity. This is one of the attractions of Paris – the capacity for accommodating anomalous and dissonant elements within its landscape, elements that anywhere else would be removed. After all, even the distinction between old and new, between the ruins of the past and the garbage of the present, was here in this area becoming increasingly vague. There were the old hovels so much appreciated by the tourists, the historical houses of the Rue Saint-Denis with their wood-wormed beams, claustrophobic and damp, falling apart. There were the prostitutes ready to pounce – now young women of a certain age who managed to lure a few desperate men. Then some solitary individual on his own, swaying as he sought his way back home. And there were even those who preferred to deny the state of things and to party. Bruno heard distinctly the music coming from an open balcony window and he could make out a few bodies as they danced. The illusion of greatness was accompanied by a solemn sense of the end. But there remained a *je ne sais quoi* of the grandiose in the decadence, in the rush towards ruin. There was something extremely sophisticated and perverse that flourished in the faces of the youngsters who shouted from the window, joyful in their own destruction. There was a time when Bruno would have found a way to procure an invitation to the party, to meet new people and to get some free drink. But now there was a stronger preoccupation that dragged him away.

The last part of Rue Saint-Denis was in bad repair and tortuous as it descended inexorably towards the river. Starting from the *faubourgs* and heading towards Medieval Paris, one had the impression of proceeding backwards in time. Soon the Roman city would come into view, or would be imagined. Some *prêt-à-porter* wholesalers, a few massage centers. An African hairdresser. There were those who slept on the streets, lying on top the ventilation ducts. In a fast-food shop a kebab spit turned, creaking mechanically. Bruno's steps became more rapid, more imperative. He headed into the more sweeping blocks surrounding Les Halles. He crossed the Place des Innocents, dominated by the marble fountain. He reached the Seine in an instant. Then, on the Pont au Change, through a light mist there appeared before Bruno a concise picture, almost a miniature model of the city.

The Louvre and the Gare d'Orsay stood out in the mist, easily recognizable. In the distance were Gothic contours, the spires and the outline of the cathedral. You could even make out the yellow glow of the Eiffel Tower. This was the much loved and celebrated city, the ideal Paris. That evening, once again, the city offered itself to him, mysterious and inviting like a woman lying under the stars. But now the stars were no longer to be seen. The river remained, threatening and dark, flowing through the looming complex of the buildings. A river, thought Bruno, was the most absurd and senseless thing you could imagine in the center of a city. It was, in the end, the most venerable monument he had met during his nocturnal walk. It represented the violent and unreasonable eruption of a natural phenomenon into a place where everything ought to be ordered and under control. But what would it have been, what would Paris be today without its river?

So Bruno leaned out over the parapet to better see the waters of the Seine. A thick and tepid fog rose up to his face, like a waft of steam. An impalpable mist confused the limits and the outlines of a normally familiar landscape. His gaze became opaque. Suddenly everything was unfathomable and distant. The form of the city, so rational up until just before, so necessary, collapsed into itself as though it had been a cardboard silhouette. Now the houses extending before him seemed to break up into an incomprehensible disorder. Down in the river the waves lapped somberly. The grey waters generated a vague noise – perhaps a mermaid's song? – and they pulled him towards them. His body, fatigued by the long walk and his fast, was suddenly as heavy as a millstone. Vertigo came over him – that sense of gravity attracting everything that exists on earth towards the ground. He gripped the parapet. He sought to resist with all his strength this strange magnetism that was pulling him down. It was five o'clock in the morning.

6.

Where to wander in Paris

The Seine, Palais-Royal, Montmartre

In this chapter I suggest three experiences, three different uses of the city and its spaces. They are three possibilities among the countless that Paris offers. The walks described here are not to be thought of as traditional tourist routes, not as strict itineraries (the classic "from point *A* to point *B*"). My intention, simply, is to provide advice and to inspire those who wish to become flâneurs. So, abandon your maps and your GPS, leave your traditional guidebooks at home. The aim is to get lost. You must feel free to wander and roam, to walk back to where you've already been, to turn right or left with no reason. When you walk in Paris you're not obliged to go to a particular place, you don't necessarily have to go shopping, you don't have to take photographs. Feel yourselves free from commitments, feel yourselves under absolutely no obligation to see a famous monument or to visit a museum. Being a flâneur means taking a real vacation from work, from your social role, from yourselves. You must abandon ordinary ideas, the journalistic and mass tourism clichés. You must sharpen the sensibilities of your spirit and your body. The city is made of paving stones and walls, of long boulevards, of trees, of shop windows, of bodies in movement and of cobbles. Paris is a living organism and, at one and the same time, it is immaterial and literary memory. The more we try to cage it within a stereotype, the more the city retreats. Paris possesses a mysterious element, an ineffable thing that cannot be predicted and cannot be easily catalogued. So do not make do with a vague or superficial knowledge – you must establish an intimate, almost physical relationship with the city.

The first place for wandering is along the Seine embankment. Each time I come back to the city after a long journey I don't really feel I have returned until I see the river. *Fluctuat nec mergitur*, "Tossed by the waves and does not sink": the coat-of-arms of Paris carries a ship navigating a river. Walking along the Seine embankment allows one to enter into deeper contact with Paris and to meditate on its history. The ideal moment for this walk is early morning, in winter if possible. It is best to avoid moments when the crowds are there, such as the later afternoon or evening, or, even worse, the days when the city council organizes musical events, shows and displays. The flâneur turns his nose up at vulgar parades of entertainment and consumerism. The water flowing through the monuments, the boats slipping by silently, the rusty jetties, these for him are the supreme spectacle. In the winter mornings the river bank is enveloped by a fine mist. The Seine flows inexorable, emitting no sound. The Seine has a thousand nuances, it reflects and refracts the colors of the sky. The boats creak, moored to the old jetties. You can smell the silt and the hum of motor cars, far off. Along the cobblestones that run along the river bank, two lovers cuddle in solitude on a bench. An old man walks slowly, taking in a timorous ray of sun. You can see the spires of the city far away, the profiles of Gothic churches and, on the horizon, the towers of the Défense.

Visit the islands of the Seine. Over the centuries almost all the islands the river possessed have been lost, joined now to the mainland. Others have been bonded together. Today three remain. The flâneur must walk them regularly to learn them by heart. The Île de la Cité is monumental and haughty: with its cathedral, the Sainte-Chapelle, the palace of justice, the hospital and the Conciergerie. It is here that the original tribes of Gaul (the Parisii) settled before their conquest by Julius Caesar and therefore before the Roman city of Lutetia was founded. Today the island is an administrative and tourist center: it has some corners of undeniable interest, such as the flower market, and some small, forgotten streets, spared by the demolitions of the 1800s. The presence of great numbers of tourists and the incessant traffic make it nonetheless the least appropriate for flânerie. The Île

Saint-Louis instead is more intimate and sheltered. It has important architectural works, such as the Hôtel Lambert and the Hôtel de Lauzun, and certainly has less traffic. The central axis of the island is special in that it allows the walking man to "isolate" himself and to wander, almost as though he's found himself in a small 1700s village far from the walls of Paris. The Île aux Cygnes, lastly, created in 1825, is in truth a spit of land in the middle of the river, linked to the mainland by three bridges. It is perhaps most appropriate for nocturnal flânerie because, thanks to its poor illumination, it offers an extraordinary view of the towers of the Front de Seine neighborhood, in the 15th arrondissement.

Visit the bridges of Paris. There are 37 bridges in the capital. We could spend hours discussing which of them offers the best view, the most majestic panorama of the city. On this matter the traditional tourist guidebooks don't skimp on suggestions and advice. In truth the flâneur develops such an intimate relationship with Paris that he has arrived at his own preferred and secret view of the city. To know with certainty which is the best would evidently mean trying each of the bridges, one by one. This would be an operation requiring several days, if not months of flânerie. After all, it would be madness to delude oneself into thinking it possible to know and to see all Paris in a few days. It is equally absurd to think that a few hours' walk might allow the visitor to know the Seine and to grasp its secrets. When you walk along the river it is therefore necessary to interrupt your stride on occasion and to walk up onto the bridges to observe the vista. The bridges are the ideal places to stop, suspended halfway, and to meditate. They are the perfect places to achieve distance from ordinary life and the quotidian. But they are also ideal places for an appointment, for waiting for a lover, or for an encounter with some solitary and melancholic woman.

The second place for wandering is Palais-Royal. Just a few meters from Rue de Rivoli, it's like a separate citadel, a garden of delights, but also a residue of what Paris was and what it should continue to be. The residence of dukes, a meeting place for the aristocracy and the people, still today housing important government institutions, Palais-Royal is an anomalous space, a strangely silent enclave, sheltered and unfashionable. Before going into the garden it's a good idea to do some reconnaissance in the streets that surround the historical princely residence like a cordon and protect it from the city: Rue de Montpensier, Rue de Beaujolais, Rue de Valois. Through the narrow lateral passages, not always easy to find, there's access to the colonnade that forms the perimeter of the garden on three sides. The solemn space of Palais-Royal is divided into two separate parts: the *place* of the Cour d'Honneur and the gardens. Under the portico once upon a time there were workshops, amusement arcades and taverns; today we have antique and designer shops, cafés and bistros. The portico, supreme example of how it is possible to transform a public space into an interior place, is the ideal location for a long, slow meditative walk.

Palais-Royal has always been one of the favorite destinations of all flâneurs. In this unusual and quiet place I have felt it possible to grasp the *genius loci*, the spirit that the ancient Romans thought of as inhabiting a place and shaping its identity. In the façades of the Palais-Royal I felt sure I had captured the essence of Parisian elegance: simple but imposing, free of exaggeration and useless decoration. In the midst of the tranquil order of the vegetation, where the energy of the fountain pulsates, I perceived the city in its eternal renewal. I saw the corrosion on the bronze decorations, the crusted, crumbling walls. I felt the ephemeral nature of the beauty and the monuments. Because Paris is still its own self; and at the same time it no longer is. Take a look at the streets surrounding the Palais-Royal; set off towards the Rue de Rivoli, towards Les Halles, and even along the Avenue de l'Opéra, and you'll see that the economic and social upheavals of the present have altered or obliterated what beauty the city possessed and what might be defined as typically Parisian. The flâneur has developed a physical relationship, almost visceral, with the city and so absorbs its malaise and its illness. If there is no flâneur in Paris who does not love the Palais-Royal profoundly, this is because we find here the registered identity, the indelible DNA of the capital. Thus love for things past derives not from melancholy, but from the quest for what remains intact, virgin, genuine.

The third place for wandering is Montmartre. Montmartre appears to the tourist as the quarter of lightheartedness and disengagement: its characteristic feature is a party air consisting of outdoor cafés, terraces, music and painters in the streets. Despite the huge numbers of visitors, it remains a predominantly residential neighborhood and is much frequented by Parisians too. Whoever visits Montmartre joins in, normally, with the procession of tourists who proceed up the hill taking small steps, painstakingly, as though each condemned to their own Calvary. The flâneur on the other hand, succeeds in breaking this chain. The *butte de Montmartre* is the highest point in Paris – a rather steep hill, which thanks to its shape allows us to engage in a more dynamic and sporty type of flânerie.

Rue Lepic, Rue des Abbesses. There is something scandalous in not following the masses, in moving against the flow. The flâneur seeks the most silent streets, cemeteries, forgotten corners where no one ever goes. It is right here that one breathes the most distant history of the neighborhood: not in the main roads, but in the side streets, in the spaces that seem to be abandoned. You see the real Montmartre in the cracks in the rendering, in the smell of fried food that sometimes arrives in wafts from the gardens. In the ivy that clings and suffocates that wall. Rue Gabrielle, Rue Drevet, Rue Berthe. Here more than ever you have to walk randomly, without worrying about taking the wrong road. You mustn't rush in reaching the top of the hill. It's best to linger, to drift, I would even say float through the streets. Rue Durantin, Rue des Trois Frères. A greengrocer, a patisserie, a liqueur shop. The beauty here is to take the steps two at a time, three at a time. Go down to the bottom of the hill; then suddenly go back up again. There are no signposts to follow – the flâneur is on a quest for the rare flower, the hidden detail that only he is able to spot. But the best of Montmartre comes at sunset, when a strange calm takes possession of its streets. Paris is down there, you can see its roofs and its spires, you can make out the indefatigable hum. This while Montmartre is still half asleep. It is then that the night bars start filling up. People flow there in search of a truce, an escape from the traffic of the city. The tourist and the dissolute head for Pigalle, toward Place de Clichy, to the variety theatres or the dubious bars. Fashionable Parisians, however, set out for Rue des Abbesses.

I have suggested three places to visit, three examples of how a flâneur can make use of the city. Although out of principle there is no single elected place to be considered better than others for practicing the noble art of flânerie, the expert in Paris will know, just as a wine-buff knows his wine, how to choose the right place at the right moment. The flâneur pays no attention to the cinema and television showgirls, he ignores the songs and the smash hits of the moment. The flâneur can also know nothing of the plots of the most famous novels, the subtleties of philosophy, and even the formulas of physics and mathematics. But he must know all the squares, all the buildings, all the parks of Paris. He must be able to recognize, instinctively, one of any of the streets in the twenty arrondissements of the capital. The flâneur is not a lighthearted tourist and neither is he an idler about town. He is a modern ascetic, the officiant of the Moment, the priest of

Appearance. He is the man who has relinquished his self, all ambition of wealth and success, in order to consecrate himself fully to the cult and the celebration of the city. Real flânerie elevates the quotidian to the sublime, renders the moment eternal. The flâneur thus has access, through the amplification of detail, to a wider vision of the urban reality. He is engaged in an infinite and impossible challenge – he would like to know and to survey every place, every episode of Paris. He would like to be able to observe the thousand destinies, the thousand stories that are woven like the warp and weft of a fabric. The solitary walking man in the city succeeds in coming out of his own self and out of his own life. This is the ultimate marvel of flânerie.

7.

Drifting along the boulevards

Grands Boulevards

Saturday, 16 January 2016. Pascal was right: all of man's misfortune comes from one thing, which is not knowing how to sit quietly in a room. This is especially true on winter afternoons, when the sun sets early, heralding a long evening with no change in the horizon. So, rather than this unbearable boredom of remaining locked up in the house, I prefer going out for a wander, roaming with no destination. I throw open the door and head in a random direction, southwards. Walking in a straight line, it would normally take me five minutes to go from my house to the Boulevard de Bonne Nouvelle. But today I intend to slacken my pace and prolong the distance in an irrational way. I zigzag, because the greatest pleasure does not consist in experiencing new things, but in savoring the infinite variation of what I already know. This exercise reaches its peak, for me, in the tiny streets, passages and courtyards that lie along the southern boundary between the 9th and 10th arrondissements. It is here that the centuries have shaped some intimate, isolated spaces, between the major avenues, where the sensation is of being in a village outside the city.

Rue Martel. Buildings set along the street like precious stones. The moonlight, lukewarm and dim, settling on the pediments. The past has vanished, yet mysteriously something of it has survived. On the pale façades, in the cracks of the rendering, on the irreparable bulging of a wall. Cours des petites écuries. Faint outlines of buildings loom, hushed and dilapidated. Somber stuccoes through the fog, and a dark doorway. It is like walking through the wings in a theatre. The "Courtyard of small stables": I cross it and shudder. Cité de Trévise. A street lamp, flickering feebly. Old enamels shining bright on the façades – still in place as if by magic. A single tree in the middle, on its own. Not a leaf falls on the cobblestones.

I am a man riding the storm, I am a drifting boat. The drift, in many respects, may be considered as the extreme level of flânerie. It is a mental and physical state that is reached under the effect of fatigue, such as comes from a long and exhausting walk, and which can be reinforced with fasting and lack of sleep. It is a state of profound disillusionment attained when one is overcome by anxiety, or when one's life aims disappear. You are drifting when you perceive the bitterness of failure and the small satisfactions of daily life no longer provide any joy. But unlike depression, the drift is accompanied by an explosion of energy, by an uncontrollable agitation that pushes you on, despite everything, to move, to seek.

I go down the Rue d'Hauteville that cuts straight through the quarter, heading south. It is a springboard towards a noisier and more pleasure-driven new world, the Grands Boulevards. Here there are historic cafés and Irish pubs, several nightclubs, the wax and chocolate museums, restaurants and fast food outlets. The crowds consist of *banlieusards*, students and office workers. In the era of the Impressionist painters, the vista of the boulevards was considered a symbol of modern life. Today, however, the experience of drifting along this boundary line – between "old Paris" to the south and the various *faubourgs* lined up on the northern side – generates the perception of traveling through an ambiguous landscape. There are many references to the district's glorious past, and not without some rather kitsch features: old signs, revival interiors and theatres remodeled in the Belle Époque style. A walk in Paris makes it possible to experience this vertiginous simultaneity: thanks to the various layers of history the city possesses, the walking man can set his life in scenes from another era.

The Grands Boulevards could be defined as a tourist district, as long as this definition does not require the presence of solely foreign visitors. I regard the tourist as the quintessential consumer, the model of a completely passive man who undertakes activities specifically designed to entertain him. The figure of the tourist perfectly embodies the sense of weariness of our times, together with a hedonistic exasperation that multiplies the number of places devoted to entertainment, to the detriment of everything else. I liken the tourists to the little dandies too, the young "hipsters" who go to the movie theaters, trendy shops and places given over to the consumption of cultural merchandise. You can recognize them with their long beards, their vintage coats, the checked shirt and showy braces. Their appearance is stilted and epicurean at one and the same time. They sit there at the tables and they discuss what might be the best night out in the city, the coolest concert or deejay of the moment. They queue up to enter a cinema or a bar. The flâneur observes the scene – he recognizes an allegory of human life. Why all this rush? Why all this anxiousness to enter the magic box of a nightclub? Isn't it, in the end, a rather unpleasant and noisy place? What are they looking for? Life is a long party with a tragic end. The flâneur is aware of all this and seeks a different kind of enjoyment, a higher form of distraction. He doesn't want to be simply the straightforward passive recipient of a concert or film. He aims to be the principal character on the urban scene, the one who enjoys to the fullest the adventures this spectacle affords.

I am now near Richelieu-Drouot. I look for a place where I can drink a beer in peace. The bars here are all conventionally bohemian. They all have a dark wood counter, a row of uncomfortable chairs and small round tables. And here are the people, the young rebels of the neighborhood. They sit in unnatural poses. They exude a cynical air. They smoke. In Paris it has become conventional to look unconventional, to the point where today's rebel in truth appears to be a person who embraces a simple, ordinary look.

Two people are talking:

"Listen, I've been wanting to talk with you about something, but I haven't had the courage to bring it up."

"Come on, Dear, I'm all ears for you."

"Last week, you know, at Johanne's birthday, I saw Paul again. I didn't want to talk to him, I'd only gone to the party to see my friends."

"Again? The Paul saga again?"

"Oh! If you'd seen him! He was really insistent. And I was drunk. We danced a bit and then I left with him. I'm really sorry, Marc. I think I've taken advantage of your patience a bit too much recently."

From the café window I observe the city of today. There is something retrograde, conservative, in the flâneur's eye. It would be imprecise to think that he loves the past to the detriment of what is new. Rather one should say that, with his holistic vision of the city, the flâneur receives with suspicion everything that is declared as being innovative and modern. There is something ridiculous in the cosmopolitanism that Paris and the Parisians like to flaunt. Come to think of it, there is nothing more ordinary, nothing flatter than what Paris is becoming today. There is nothing exciting about the slow conversion of Paris into a generic city.

The Parisians vaunt their having their fingers on the pulse, their being fashionable and so cool. But Paris is no longer the center of the new: what one perceives on the city's streets, for example in the vista of the Grands Boulevards, is simply the "background radiation" of the modern, the local presence of the global. I sense it in the big chain stores that become steadily more frequent as I get closer to the Opéra, in the offices of foreign banks and insurance companies, in the sham Breton, Japanese, Italian restaurants. Paris was a book to be read. But the Paris of today resembles one of those instant books, consumer books that are meant to be gulped down in a rush. It is a novel that recounts many destinies, many intertwined stories. It is an encyclopedia that seeks to tell us a bit about everything, but in a rather superficial and vague way. The idea of the city as a work of art, as ultimate perfection, almost the manifesto of a civilization – as Haussmann's Paris was – has run its course. Paris was a "world": now it appears to me as a compendium of all possible worlds, a catalogue of human diversity. Perhaps in the near future a human being without history, without identity, will walk these streets? I look at the shop windows, the advertising and the signs in succession along the boulevard – it would seem that today's society magnifies this lightness of identity, encouraging the prospect of a future city consisting largely of hotels, traversed by generic individuals, devoid of ethnic and sexual connotations.

The second beer.

"It's up to you now to accept your limitations.

You have to recognize your own problems and try to sort them out on your own, like a grown up."

"Please, Love, keep your voice down! Everyone will hear us."

"Listen, I think it's best if we just finish it here. Your attitude really irritates me. You behave like a little boy. Or now I think about it, like my father."

"Don't be like that, Love! If I've hurt your feelings, I apologize."

"Enough of your melodrama. I'm going now, going out with my friends …"

I set off walking again. I move quickly, unhindered, like a billiard ball rolling through the city. Paris is a flat city. Paris is "any city". Even the men and women I come across all seem to tell me the same story, driven by more or less the same goals. These are very simple desires, almost the same for everyone. Sometimes they are expressed uncouthly, sometimes in the guise of high ideals. Everyone seeks desperately to emerge, to stand out from the crowd, and it is precisely this absurd effort that makes them all desperately the same. The Parisian crowd is an allegory of the world and there is something exemplary about it. Paris is beautiful, but it can also offer the gloomiest, the most chilling spectacle anyone has ever seen. In the arena of the boulevard, everyone wants to be first, seeking to make their own space in the world. One's own happiness seems to depend on the ability to jostle, to get ahead of the others.

I have to find a way out. The solution, for the flâneur, is not a matter of differentiating oneself from the others, but of vanishing. I decide now to let myself be guided by the disordered motions of the crowd. Maybe anyone who wanders aimlessly at length through the great city really does feel he is something of a detective and something of a "man of the crowd", like the protagonist of Poe's story. My movement stems from an insatiable curiosity for the beauty of the world, for the fascination of the modern city. Yet, deep inside, I harbor, as does any walking man, a darker and deeper desire: to escape from my inner self and merge my being with the world around me. Because if the spectacle of the city is infinitely rich – and I love analyzing the faces, the gait and the clothes of the passers by – there are days when the greatest pleasure in my flânerie consists simply of disappearing into the crowd and forgetting myself. Surrounded by the multitude, I enjoy the anonymity, that feeling of emptiness and impunity that the great city can give me. So, under the garish lights of the Grand Rex cinema, in the midst of the tide of unknown women and men, of passers by with a thousand faces, today I follow my true vocation – getting lost. I do not lose my way, as fools or tourists do; but instead I lose myself and find release for a few hours from the cumbersome weight of my own ego.

8.

The ruins of Paris

> *Old Paris is no more (the form of a city changes more quickly, alas! than the human heart)*
>
> (Charles Baudelaire, *Tableaux parisiens*)

Paris is a city to be read. It is a book in which the history of humanity sediments, like geological eras. Reading Paris is the joy and the pastime of the flâneur. During a walk in the French capital one can move in time and space simultaneously. But faced with the urban transformations that modernization has brought and brings, the flâneur adopts an ambiguous attitude. The flâneur is secretly joyful about the metamorphosis of the urban landscape, because it introduces new elements that can stimulate his imagination. There exists, however, a stereotype, a recurring theme, associated in various historical periods with the topic of flânerie: the mourning for the inexorable transformation and disappearance of the historic city. It is probable that the origin of this stereotype or literary *topos* is to be found precisely in the identification of the flâneur in the city. The walking man in Paris recognizes in the history of the city his own vanished past and he regrets this loss.

The theme of the ruins of Paris dates from the Second Empire, at the time of the *grands travaux* designed and directed by Baron Haussmann, the "destroyer" artist. In striving to make of the French capital the emblem of the modern metropolis it was indeed necessary to obliterate part of its urban fabric, the Medieval city above all. Haussmann's work constituted an epochal moment even for his contemporaries. The many articles that appeared in the newspapers of the time are testimony to this fact, together with the debates that followed their publication. Further evidence is provided in paintings and in the continual references to the transformation of the city's planning that we find in documents and novels. Some texts even discuss the "end" of Paris – *Paris démoli, mosaïque de ruines* (1853) by Eduard Fournier, or the *Ruines de Paris* (1858) by Charles Monselet. The notion of ruins also holds a prominent place in Baudelaire's *Tableaux parisiens*, fundamental evidence in understanding the sensibility of man and artist in the modern city. In particular in the poem, "Le Cygne", published in 1861, the relationship between urban landscape and the author's inner self is established. The demolition of the city thus becomes an allegory for the transient nature of things:

> Paris changes! but naught in my melancholy
> Has stirred! New palaces, scaffolding, blocks of stone,
> Old quarters, all become for me an allegory,
> And my dear memories are heavier than rocks.

This poem later became an essential reference for French authors who recognized a reflection of their personal experiences in the urban landscape and its incessant morphing. Right from the start of the epoch of Haussmann-style modernity, many authors made reference to the practice of flânerie, not without a nostalgic flavor, as an act of resistance to the transformation of the city. Consider, for example the project undertaken by Eugène Atget, an important early twentieth-century exponent of urban photography, who tried to capture those corners of a Paris that were then in decay. If it was the never-ending transformation of the city that made it a source of artistic inspiration, however, the theme of the end of flânerie overlaps with the actual practice of flânerie, as much among the Surrealist authors as in those who had more recently resurrected the experience: this is the case, for example, with Jacques Réda and his *Ruines de Paris* (1977).

The great economic and social upheavals in the latter half of the twentieth century upset the shape of the city to such an extent that the topic of the ruins of Paris came to the fore again. The topic was present in much criticism – from the postwar period onwards – of contemporary town planning and the economic structure that it represented. In the wake of the Lettrist movement and the COBRA group, the Situationist International, founded in Paris in 1957, shifted attention towards the balance of power between politics and urban spaces, transforming aimless walking into a political gesture and a form of resistance against the "control strategies" of industrial society. Guy Debord, leader of this movement, was a critic both of the privatization and standardization inflicted on the urban spaces of the French capital. Debord also identifies a general movement of "isolation" as a feature of postwar town planning, stripping the city of its interesting and characteristic features, decentralizing the working classes and concentrating services in distinct areas separate from the old residential centers. Starting in the '70s, the physical disappearance of the traditional city became, not only in France but, more generally, in the western world, a widespread motif in the imagery of literature and films and gave rise to disturbing and dystopian representations of the city of the future. Consider, for example, the descriptions of Trude and Pentesilea in Calvino's *Città invisibili* (1972) or the Los Angeles in which Ridley Scott's *Blade Runner* (1982) is set, or even the novels of James G. Ballard: the formal expression of the postmodern city appears to be a patchwork of over-full or over-empty spaces that are undefined or even virtual, as in *City of Bits* by William J. Mitchell (1995).

On the critical front, architectural scholars and sociologists have suggested that the metropolis of today may no longer be able to perform the function of the traditional city, nor permit the freedom of movement that flânerie requires. Melvin M. Webber, in his studies of the organizational structures of megalopolises, was the first to use the term "non-places" in *Explorations into Urban Structure* (1964). With specific regard to the Parisian situation, in 1992 Marc Augé defined the "non-place", as opposed to an anthropological place, as "a space that can be defined as neither identity-creating nor relational nor historic."(Augé 1992, p. 100.) According to the French anthropologist, consumerist society produces non-places that do not integrate with the historic city and create neither identity nor relationships between individuals but only loneliness and monotonous uniformity. These are car parks, airports, motorways, major railway stations, supermarkets, fast food outlets and chains of international hotels and shops, both products and emblems of a technologically advanced society, characterized by greater mobility than the past and by other phenomena linked to urbanization and mass migration. Non-places are the physical evidence of a crisis in identity and interpersonal relationships, because they do not function as symbolic centers or landmarks for community members. They are facilities designed to be passed through and used, an expression of a world designed for lonely individuality, for the transitory, the temporary and the ephemeral: "spaces that are overcrowded and abruptly deserted, but never inhabited". They are both cause and epiphenomenon of a global standardization of customs and everyday life under the banner of consumption. Aiming for the greatest degree of practicality and economy, spaces in the city are "standardized", to the point that even Paris verges on being one of the many global cities that "resemble their airports".

In his essay *The Generic City* (1995), the Dutch architect Rem Koolhass provides a description of an indeterminate city that consists entirely of non-places. It does not really have a periphery because it has no center; its architecture is impressive due to the originality and the beauty of its buildings, but consists mostly of empty spaces, anonymous and deserted. Oblivious to its own history, the generic city looks like a compendium of anthropological diversity and yet, despite being a symbol of global standardization, its landscape is scarred by antithetical elements and strong opposing forces. It's not just a question of differences due to specific functions in each district and to social inequality. Rather, according to Koolhass, what we see here is a predisposition towards striking contrasts, for disjointed spaces and distinct breaks, as well as a stylistic pursuit, modeled on postmodernist pastiche, which aims to highlight the differences and eccentricity of individual buildings. Contrast then becomes the dominant feature of the urban landscape and it is no surprise to see dragons or Buddhist temples in a shopping center, or a shanty town at the foot of the towers of finance.

9.

A dangerous game

Pont Neuf

The Game is played primarily with the eyes: observing the vista of the city, the irresistible tableau of modern beauty, to the point of discovering the superficial in the profound, spotting the profound in the superficial. The Game is a way of walking, a way of taking control in the urban space. In the player's eyes, walls become open doors. The most solid edifices appear as if they were built on sand. The city is sinuous and tiring, the city is alive. The city is there to be traversed and caressed like a female body. Paris appears to us like the embodiment of our desires and our cravings. But the player is constantly unsatisfied, trapped in the eternal present of the aesthetic life. As much as he tries to chase it with all his energy, the city remains elusive. Paris contains every experience imaginable, it always offers something more than the individual can experience. Thus the player exhausts himself in aimless desire. His life seems like a series of distractions, of moments set side by side that do not form a story. And yet the player has a line of conduct, he has a plan. An amorous encounter is the pinnacle towards which whoever walks alone in the city secretly aspires.

I learnt about the Game in different ways. I mixed with the Parisian "pick-up artists" who I met in the bars, parks and streets of the capital. I read the books that form the basis of the discipline of the pick-up, i.e. the art of seducing women met in day-to-day situations. And so I discovered a link that ties the Parisian literary tradition with the most mundane of manuals that tell you how to obtain the phone number of a passing girl. I then dedicated myself to the activity. I believe the pick-up artists have developed an altogether unique relationship with the city space, reminiscent in some respects of the nineteenth-century practice of flânerie. I am referring, in particular, to the so-called "street game", in other words hitting on unknown women on the streets of the city, an activity that has been considered by many as the most difficult and the zenith of the art of the pick-up.

Summer 2014, a sunny day in Place Dauphine. I am alone, ready for chance, for the unexpected. I prefer a neutral style, avoiding the untidy look as much as I avoid looking too smart. My aim – it might seem strange – is not to get myself noticed, but to observe the crowd. I single out the object of my desire among the mass of moving bodies. I try to guess the age and occupation of the passing women and reconstruct their life stories through the few clues on offer. I am crossing the Pont Neuf, the oldest stone bridge in Paris. I find myself outside the city, halfway between two worlds. To the north I can hear the bustle of the industrious and working-class Right Bank. To the south the Left Bank is drowsy, we think of it as spoiled and somewhat pretentious. Around its halfway point, the bridge crosses the Île de la Cité and opens out onto the triangular Place Dauphine. In this noble but run-down square, the stuccoes shine with a macabre light. The fabulous decoration and the nudes on the pediments excite me. The paint on the doorways flaking like dried lips. The dark river glides below, the river that attracts vacationers but also suicides. The Seine evokes the passage of time and death. From this perspective, the shape of the city is always beautiful, but somehow shrouded in haze. Then, when the eye seems to be sated with the vista before it, the figure of a woman appears in front of me. She moves forward, exhibiting a suspicious self-confidence. She startles the old stones of the bridge. Her gait is assertive, to cope with the hostility of the world. But the expression on her face, as far as I can make out, is gentle and lonely. Hovering above her fullness of form is an intimation of vulnerability, of finality, that kindles desire more than ever. Maybe she too, returning from work, has fantasized about an encounter that will shatter the daily routine or perhaps she is thinking of something else entirely. This is when I step forward and speak to her.

 When you stop a girl in the street, you put your

whole self to the test. First of all, you have to work out a precise opening gambit, in the most appropriate language and register. You have to choose between a contextual approach, in which you try to create an incident that will initiate a conversation – a request for information, a photograph or something else – and a more direct and natural approach: "I was sitting there and saw you go by; I said to myself that if I didn't come and talk to you, I wouldn't get a second chance." The words are uttered calmly, together with the right gestures. There is an exciting tension in this scene. Everything is decided in just seconds. The difficulty, after exchanging a few words, is in creating a pretext that leads from this encounter to a potential and necessary follow-up. It is possible, after a brief conversation, that she will want to continue on her way or, alternatively, decide to change her schedule and stay with you. Much depends not only on how you look and what you say, but above all on how well you have been able to read her signs of approval or rejection and how well you have managed to attune your mood to hers. If the girl is in a hurry or has no intention of following you at that moment, you just ask for her number and then vanish into the crowd like a bandit.

As with flânerie, the Game is an exercise in freedom and is an awareness particularly immune to theorization; it is hard to confine it to definite phrases or a speech. It is an almost esoteric form of knowledge, which can only be partially expressed or conveyed in writing. The manuals, for example, have lessons on how to conduct an exchange of messages in the right way to get a date; they explain how to overcome a woman's uncertainty and how to handle the infamous "last-minute resistance". These techniques, drawing inspiration even from neuro-linguistic programming, are just partial truths, never objective. Seduction requires other – more interior – qualities. The Game, indeed, is an existential choice: it is not a playful activity or a simple pastime, but a discipline that governs your life.

In the context of seduction, the street game represents a "Copernican revolution", because it assumes a whole new relationship with the female sex and with the spaces of the city. The pick-up artist is an alpha male, but he is also a subversive. He runs counter to common sense and to what literary and cultural tradition has taught us. The pick-up artist distances himself from the "gentleman", who has an obsequious attitude towards women and puts them on a sort of pedestal, doing everything possible, in other words, to ensure she'll never play along. The Game instead teaches us not to focus on the object of desire or on one woman in particular, but rather on constructing one's own personality. While the average man has a passive attitude to his existence and tends to shelter behind the concept of fate or coincidence, the player takes control of his own life. The player is not the one who harasses girls when drunk on a Saturday night. He looks with commiseration and pity on other men who wear themselves out in the morass of dating sites or at dance or cookery classes. He is not even the heir to Casanova, the libertine of Enlightenment inspiration, who sees the amorous encounter as a sophisticated exchange of sexual favors. With regard to today's world, in which sexuality is understood as a commodity (an idea reflected in the institution of the "one-night stand", of Anglo-Saxon origin), the player maintains an aesthetic and moral superiority. Rather, he is a follower of a figure from a Romantic background – Don Juan, the seducer who flouts social mores and leads the women he meets, as well as himself, to a more profound and more carnal experience.

There is something both terrible and heroic in the player's character. He is driven by a mysterious force. He is stuck in the endless search for his own perfection. What is the ideal place in a city at a given time of day? What is the positioning of his hands, the expression at the corner of his mouth, the allusion or joke that will make the chosen one succumb? Some purists no longer even sleep with the women they pick up; they have internalized the Game to such an extent as to consider it a contest with their own selves, an entirely inner enterprise. Then they impose constraints or obstacles so that the challenge still proves exciting. At that point the Game becomes a daily challenge that traps the individual in a dynamic of improvement from which he can no longer escape. Thus the player ends up being stuck in his city and his desperate routine, rejecting everything else. The player's strength stems effectively from a detailed knowledge and control of the urban territory. Contemporary society has a tendency to confine the territory of seduction to areas, both actual and virtual, that are understood to be for "picking up" and that make a fortune out of men's frustrations, i.e. dating sites, vacation resorts and nightclubs. In these, the man starts at a distinct disadvantage. When he is reduced to the role of consumer he tends in effect to adopt a subordinate position to the woman. The street, however, is a place where this balance of power is reversed. In the overcrowded metropolis, public spaces are the scene of open combat. Paris is a battlefield where you have to fend off the crowd or even shoulder your way through. The looks of passers-by undress the woman and slice through her body like invisible sword-strokes.

In the literary field, it seems to me that the relationship the pick-up artist has with spaces in the city corresponds to a typically Parisian tradition, in which the street is regarded as a primary meeting place and the female passer-by becomes an object of interest, or even the main source of inspiration, for the artist-flâneur. Paris is the city of the Revolution, of drifting and of flânerie. Paris is also, *par excellence*, the city of the street game, of the *drague de rue*. It would take a long time to retrace the historical evolution of this practice that has now become a cultural tradition. A starting point could perhaps be the nocturnal wanderings that the libertine writer Rétif de la Bretonne describes in *Les Nuits de Paris* (1788). But it is during the nineteenth century, with the urban crowd becoming predominant and thus the flâneur becoming established, that a new female figure began to spread in the common and literary imaginary – the female passer-by. She represents a break with the abstract and ideal image of the woman-angel that in the western literary canon is the muse of the lovestruck sweetheart poet. The flâneur's woman is not the beautiful courtesan, but is the passer-by. She is the embodiment of the ideal of fleeting and desultory beauty that Baudelaire placed at the foundation of modern art. The female passer-by symbolizes the sense of the possible that is associated with life in the metropolis. Like the "painter of modern life" described by Baudelaire, the player identifies and, from all the available sensory stimuli, selects the detail that is important to him: a bare ankle, the bounce of a breast or the fold of a dress.

It is precisely the transitory nature of female beauty – a rare and unrepeatable beauty that few will know how to take advantage of – that increases its value in his eyes. The idea of a chance meeting in the maze of the city was an important theme for the Surrealist authors. The novel *Nadja* (1926) for example, by André Breton, was inspired by an encounter with an unknown woman passing by on the streets of Paris. The Surrealist idea that chance dominates the course of life is in contrast, however, with the *modus operandi* of the player, who acts observing rigid rules and applying an experimental, almost scientific method. Although urban exploration does not necessarily have an erotic goal, for many flâneurs the image of the city and that of the woman end up being superimposed. Remaining in the Parisian context, think, for example, of the authors of the Oulipo group, for whom the calculation and obsessive classification of the city's physical elements – possibly a means of keeping a volatile world like the urban one under control – led to an almost voyeuristic contemplation of Paris and its crowds. The effort that drives us to understand and decipher the text of the city goes hand in hand with a desire for self-dissipation, a Dionysian breakdown of individuality, which finds its outlet in erotic activity.

The way the player faces up alone to the multitude can inspire, there is no denying it, a certain admiration. Nevertheless, his activity is highly immoral. There is something immoral in the cynicism, in the lack of compassion. There is something indecent in the behavior of the player, in the fact that he appears suddenly, upsets the lives of others, and then just as suddenly vanishes. At the same time, the hypothesis put forward by some critics in the context of Gender Studies – under which areas of the modern city and their established uses are the projection of a sexist vision – does not seem totally unfounded. Just consider, for example, that if someone is talking about "street-walkers", he is probably not referring to flâneuses (female flâneurs), but to prostitutes, the embodiment *par excellence* of women as sex objects. The player represents perfectly this sexist mentality and, at the same time, applies to amorous relationships the cumulative and reifying logic that characterizes contemporary consumer society. The player is a close relative of the flâneur since both evolved in the same environment, the modern city, characterized by individualism and an exasperated spirit of competition. The player is a character who is terminally ill with all the ills of our century, but in some respects he is also the hero of our times. He is an obsessive-compulsive neurotic who tries with every means possible to dominate nature and fate, to give a logical form to the most instinctive and emotive component of human existence. The player is a man who has pushed the paradoxes of our society to the extreme level, at his own peril.

The life of the player is fascinating, but it is also desperate. There is something too brief in the instant. There is something absurd in spending one's entire life in celebrating the ephemeral. The player seeks to fill the long silence of his interior life, deluding himself that the petty things he has lived are grand and lasting, that there exists a sort of eternal return. And so the moment of fatigue arrives. The moment in which everyone's life should appear no longer as a random flow of events, but as a story to be told, a narration to be unfolded. That day, thinking again about existence in its entirety, thinking again about the events of his life, even the smallest, the player too seems to perceive a sense, a form of predestination. The same errors, the hesitations, sit now within a wider project. There were no coincidences. Indeed, even those choices that initially had seemed to be false steps, terrible mistakes, acquire another meaning and everything is reconciled in a supreme synthesis that is the story of life. This is the moment in which the Game ends and the ethical life begins.

10.

The city of tomorrow

Tour Eiffel, Disneyland Paris

> *A real crocodile can be found in the zoo, and as a rule it is dozing or hiding, but Disneyland tells us that faked nature corresponds much more to our daydream demands.*
>
> (Umberto Eco,
> *Dalla periferia dell'impero*)

For those who take an interest in the history of the flâneur and the habit of walking in the city, Paris is a particularly attractive field of study because it is possible to revisit the evolution of areas of consumerism in the course of a single walk, from the arcades to those multifunctional buildings that I shall call "super-places".[2] Spared the bombings of the Second World War and despite some major post-war transformation, Paris has retained the coherence of the city of the past. The result is a sharp divide between the physical landscape of the city (cityscape) and the cultural landscape (mindscape), profoundly influenced by the modern. Paris today is also marked by the duality between the center and the suburbs (*banlieues*), a conflict that the authorities have been trying for years to alleviate. The mentality and habits of the masses, like the transport system, have been influenced by the particularly dense and centripetal structure of the metropolis. Despite all this, today in the center of Paris it is still possible to experience an urban *promenade* that if not identical, is at least comparable with that of the nineteenth-century flâneur. Anyone, however, who decides to go beyond the ring road (*boulevard periphérique*), the highway encircling the historic city like an outer circle of walls, to head towards the department of Seine-Saint-Denis, for example, or towards the airport at Roissy, will find a decidedly different architectural and human landscape. They will find there the tedious expanse of the new city, the railway junctions, waste grounds and car graveyards, and even a mysterious blue cuboid shape, the Ikea shop at Villiers-sur-Marne, like a spaceship from some distant planet. In this suburban limbo, which appears scattered and insubstantial, there are many examples of super-places: not just the malls and the

---

[2] For the use of this term, see the catalogue of the exhibition held in Bologna in 2007: Agnoletto et al. 2007.

airport but also, for example, the La Défense business district and the Disneyland Paris amusement park.

As new points of attraction for the urban masses, the super-places stand out in the Parisian landscape due to their impressive scale, the variety of functions they perform and the multitude of people who visit them. Unlike non-places, they assert a strong identity and a power of attraction; they stand out as landmarks that dominate the area in which they are located, at the same time bringing about a break with the historical city. The prefix "super-" puts the emphasis on their multipurpose function and at the same time sets them apart from non-places: rather than marginal areas in the city landscape, they have emerged as icons of a new centrality. The distinctive characteristic of the super-place is its ability to dominate the area to which it belongs, catalyzing crowds and guiding their movements. This is a faculty that derives as much from the super-place's economic weight as from its intrinsic symbolic power. The super-places and especially the great shopping malls that we find on the outskirts of Paris, as in other world metropolises, could be therefore seen as an evolution of what Benjamin defined as "phantasmagorias": aesthetic incarnations of an economic and technical model, images of itself that a society wants to present through the medium of merchandise and its ostentatious display (Benjamin 1982). The word "phantasmagoria" underlines, however, the fetishism or, more literally, the "animation" that merchandise is subject to, where the symbolic value tends to outweigh the market value. Benjamin traces the origin of the phantasmagoria, and hence the election of merchandise as a symbol, to the Parisian *passages*, opened in the first half of the nineteenth century, designed effectively as drawing rooms or "cabinets of curiosities", contrasting with the deterioration of a city that would have to wait much longer for Haussmann's modernization plans. A further stage was reached with the first *grands magasins*, such as the Bon Marché, opened in 1867 on the Left Bank of the Seine: a building completely separate from the outside world, where the products were exhibited in an open space in which customers could circulate freely. Bon Marché was even equipped, for the first time, with a toilet reserved for the ladies and a reading room. Finally, world expositions – invented at the height of the second Industrial Revolution to highlight technical progress under the auspices of utilitarian ethics and to give fresh impetus to trade and commerce – became gradually, towards the end of the nineteenth century, the realm of the spectacularly marvelous, compendiums of everything different that the industrial world had to offer. The Paris Exposition of 1889, with the construction of the Eiffel Tower as its finishing touch, marked the transformation of international trade fairs into amusement parks and celebrated a new architecture devoted to spectacular superfluity. For this reason the Exposition may be considered the forerunner or prototype for the super-places that would emerge towards the end of the following century.

The study of amusement parks makes it possible to understand what became of the practice of flânerie in mass society, since retail spaces tend to follow the same logic as amusement parks. This is the experience described in 1975 by Umberto Eco in *Travels in Hyperreality*, an account of a visit to the great American amusement parks. According to Eco, as an allegory of the consumer society but also a place of total passivity, Disneyland aims to reconstruct "a fantasy world more genuine than the real thing". Modern man's fulfilment seems to be found in the simulation of another, more opulent and spectacular reality, rather than in interaction with the real world. This dimension, over and above the distinction between dreams and reality, is defined by Eco as "hyperreality".[3] The spectacle offered to amusement park visitors – and which constitutes the sign, in semiotics – is not confined to representing reality, but ultimately replaces it. In hyperreality, therefore, the sign aspires to be the thing itself so that the distance between the real world and imaginable worlds is eliminated.

Established as a vital cog in the economy of the entire Paris region, Disneyland Paris – the largest theme park in the old continent – represents the emblem of a process affecting many tourist sites in the French capital. Indeed, it is not only shopping centers that are invested with symbolic value and turned into theme parks but also, conversely, sites of historic or cultural interest that are converted into retail spaces, to the extent that visitors will have trouble appreciating the difference between the main street in Disneyland Paris and the main street of Bercy Village, for example.

[3] A term subsequently revived in Baudrillard 1981.

Disneyland Paris represents an alternative to reality, equivalent to the concept of hyperreality depicted by Eco: it aims to create an imaginary dimension that will gradually replace the real world. It is no longer a question of staving off the tedium of a summer afternoon with a visit to a children's playground, but rather entering a daydream, a world that is more rewarding than everyday life. It is no surprise that nowadays some tourists no longer choose to spend their holidays in Paris but directly at Disneyland, making a foray into the historic city perhaps, to check out the Arc de Triomphe or the Eiffel Tower. Visiting Disneyland Paris is like being confronted with what Venturi prophesied in *Learning from Las Vegas* (1972) – a book regarded as a manifesto of postmodern architecture – which recommends the city of Nevada as a model for future town planning decisions. But if Disneyland and Las Vegas were imitating Paris, now it is Paris, at least in its tourist center, that imitates Disneyland: the paradigm of a city freed from its traditional functions and consecrated to pure entertainment.

If we observe the behavior of the crowds in shopping malls and amusement parks, we might now think that flânerie has become today a widespread social practice and that the shopper or tourist represents, in some respects, an evolution of the nineteenth-century flâneur. In this sense, the nineteenth-century *passages*, Haussmann's Paris and the new phantasmagorias of consumerism fall into the same experiential category. Indeed, if the flâneur was driven by a desire to escape from himself, epitomized by the man of the crowd, the ritual of shopping could be evidence of a desperate search for a *divertissement* as the only possible horizon in the post-metaphysical world. The nineteenth-century solitary walking man, however, as critical and detached observer of the urban scene, sought nevertheless to decipher or "read" this spectacle: his aimless wandering was in contrast to the bustling movement of the crowd. Freedom of movement and critical awareness are, however, conditions that are more difficult to achieve in twenty-first century shopping malls, where the architectural and thematic elements are designed to elicit a particular effect, to suggest a range of emotions and guide individuals and their attention along predefined routes, providing, at most, an illusion of freedom.

Referencing the practice of wandering through the city, some contemporary artists have shown an interest in those interstices or marginal areas that have eluded the processes of spectacularization and commodification characterizing places dedicated to consumerism. It would be superfluous to point out the role of the suburban areas as a source of inspiration or field of investigation for the artist-flâneurs. From *Monuments of Passaic*, a summary of Robert Smithson's experience in an abandoned industrial suburb of New Jersey in 1967, to the adventures of Iain Sinclair along London's M25 orbital motorway, up to the documentaries and studies that have proliferated in recent years following the pioneering work of the Chicago School, with the emergence of the suburbs as a recurring theme in urban studies debates. Restricting the discussion to the Parisian context, it was the Surrealist avant-garde that introduced the experimentation of suburban flânerie. In May 1924, Aragon, Breton, Morise and Vitrac randomly marked the route they intended to follow on a road map of France: this was the road between the towns of Blois and Romorantin, about 200 kilometers south of Paris. It was precisely the absolute pointlessness of such a journey, far from the tourist circuits or shopping streets of any importance, that freed the travellers from the imperative of productivism and created the conditions for capturing the wonders of the quotidian, which was the basis of inspiration for Surrealist art. The Situationists, in their turn, experimented with alternative routes within and without the center of Paris. In more recent years the thorny question of the Parisian *banlieues* has been tackled many times, both in political and sociological debate and in literary and cinematographic production, to the extent that it would be superfluous to deal with it here again. I shall limit myself, however, to mentioning two works by Jean Rolin, *Zones* (1995) and *La Clôture* (2002), because, by means of suburban flânerie, they tackle the problem of the Parisian *banlieues* without the clamor and the instrumentalization in a political key that often accompanies these topics. Rolin, a professional reporter, explores the spaces that surround the historic heart of Paris, recording the signs of the profound transformation, not only in terms of planning but primarily in social and anthropological terms, that France experienced in the post-war period. Rolin found a resurgence of re-vindication of identity, often in violent forms. He photographed the dark side of the "assimilation" program sponsored by the French government, but also the emergence of the stark differences between the various ethnic and cultural groups that make up the mosaic of Paris today.

These experiences of wandering and exploring the suburban areas seem to signal the end of the utopian depictions of the city as ecumene and "global village" and dispel the prophecies, in vogue towards the end of the twentieth century, predicting the physical demise of the city. After all, as Manuel Castells writes, "The global city is not a place but a process." (Castells 1996, p. 146.) Rather than the process of suspension of identity and standardization that was supposed to characterize the metropolis of the future – in the literary imaginary as in some sociological studies – experiences of flânerie through the suburban sprawl seem to highlight new social unrests and tensions in the contemporary metropolis. Far from being non-places or global villages, the Parisian *banlieues*, like those of other world metropolises, seem to be asserting themselves as "territories" *par excellence* – the weak link in the world order. Indeed, the conflicts that emerge from sociological analysis find parallels in the spatial organization and distribution of structures or buildings for which clear division from the spaces surrounding them becomes an essential prerequisite to their functioning.

11.

Shopping as one of the fine arts

La Défense

Tuesday, 16 February 2016. La Défense, Passerelle de l'Arche. Silence at last. I leave behind me the routine monotony of Courbevoie. To the right there is a cemetery, to the left the site of a new stadium under construction. Today I am visiting Europe's largest business quarter using the back door: it's the artists' entrance. With a certain gravitas I climb the marble staircase of the "Grande Arche". I go past the glass screens that decorate the top. Before me a surreal landscape takes shape, caressed by a breeze. The Esplanade de la Défense looks like a montage of fragments, a collage of contemporary architecture compressed into a chimerical space, separated from the city center. It certainly cannot claim the dizzy heights of the Asian metropolises, but the density of the La Défense buildings is so great as to give this cluster of towers a significant upward lift. The fact that the buildings sit on a separate platform, raised above street level, accentuates the alienating effect. Despite being aligned on the city's historical axis of development and the fact that its arch interacts with the arch of the Arc de Triomphe, and that of the Louvre, La Défense conveys an immediate effect of schism and acceleration.

The flâneur has mixed feelings regarding modernity. For example, I don't like isolated towers – the hostile Tour Montparnasse for example – and yet I remain in admiration in front of a large and compact cluster of skyscrapers. I know that those who work in them have little in common with me, a flâneur, and that these buildings represent a form of power – just look at the names of the companies who occupy them – that goes beyond the strictly economic sphere. Yet on days when I want to escape the traffic-congested streets of the city, I love the impressive spectacle of these silent skyscrapers, because they embody a Promethean challenge. They are the new towers of Babel, monuments to human hubris. There are days when I simply cannot bear the anachronistic streets of central Paris, those that express a sort of noble equilibrium and monarchical order. At La Défense, however, what is on display is the clash of the titans, the competitive dynamic that forms the basis of capitalist civilization. When I sit on the steps of the Grande Arche and contemplate the view of La Défense, I feel I have before me an allegory of the modern world. The earliest towers at La Défense, those erected in the 1960s and '70s, pursued the imperative of functionalism, manifesting themselves as pure and elemental geometric forms. Over the course of the following decades, the landscape of the business quarter has been added to with more complex and original constructions. The architectural style has shown a continuous emancipation of form, in harmony with an architecture in which "form follows function", the expression of an economic system that wants to be unfettered by rules and moral principles.

At 12:15, people begin to leave their offices and rush towards the restaurants and fast food outlets. I stand up and go down the marble staircase. The details of the street furniture and some buildings of La Défense, which was at one time considered futuristic, today look rather dated. Because of the excessively high rents, some companies have chosen to abandon the business quarter and build their own out-of-town campus. Maybe the details are not important, though; these spaces are made to be crossed at great speed. You have to put yourself in the shoes of the businessman in suit and tie, who has no time and is the antithesis of the flâneur. Apart from their lunch break, after all, any off duty office workers aiming to be flâneurs on the parvis of La Défense have to justify their inactivity by producing at least a cigarette or a mobile phone. Even at La Défense, however, there is a preferred place, an oasis in which the experience of flânerie is not just tolerated but even encouraged. This is Les Quatre

Temps, the largest shopping mall in France, which stands just a few meters south of the Grande Arche.

The landscape created by contemporary urban planning seems to be marked by the aesthetics of contrast. Les Quatre Temps has a glazed rectangular form but with no windows, a separate environment from the world, which remains confined outside. Inside the shopping mall, the ideal temperature conditions, the lighting system and the artificial ventilation create an abstract and unreal climate. What it offers the visitor, guided by the signs that form part of the scenery and by deliberately aroused sensations, is a "synesthetic" experience. You walk through these cocooned and fluid spaces as if under the influence of a sedative. The abundance of food, the smell of the goods, the background music and the hypnotic motion of the crowd both attract and reassure the spectator. Facilities like these are designed not just for the purchase and consumption of goods, but above all for the "enjoyment" of experiences, so that the imperative *I'm going in order to buy* becomes *I'm buying in order to go*. Relieved of any commitment or moral precept, the consumer experiences a state of suspension, where the only dimension that counts is the present, the present of individual needs and desires that require immediate satisfaction. On reflection, the force of attraction of these retail spaces seems to be linked to the possibility of an escape from reality: they are configured as imaginary refuges in contrast with anything negative the external environment may contain, including loneliness. The large retail spaces or super-places represent not just the agora, but also the acropolis of today's city. They are the grandiose sanctuaries of contemporary nihilism, where those who are lost and alone find refuge.

When you go to a shopping mall it is necessary to have an at least indefinite idea of what you would like to buy. This idea serves if nothing else to justify to yourself that going to the temple of shopping is absolutely indispensable. I too, today, had built myself an excuse: the plan, as yet rather vague, was to buy myself a tie. Not only do I not know how to knot a tie, but I don't know how to match one to other clothes. But possessing such an accoutrement would be for me something new, something exceptional. My style, normally, is rather casual. Now I'm looking for an accessory to wear on those special occasions, to impress someone or to amaze my friends. After having wandered for a good half an hour with the intention of sounding out the territory, I finally decide to enter a shop, a megastore belonging to an international chain. The customers are all excited and noisy. The men's department, unfortunately, occupies a marginal position and the choice is not as wide-ranging as I had hoped for. I choose two ties anyway and go to the changing room. There is a real crush and a lack of air that renders the experience quite unpleasant. And then it seems to me that the excessively casual style of these ties, which do not appear to be of good quality, is not suitable for me and the serious role I would like to play with this accessory. I leave the megastore and begin walking again. To boost my energy levels I have a snack, a sort of industrial-style ice-cream. I wander several times from one floor to another of the shopping mall. I like the escalators; I enjoy the sensation of mindlessness that they provide because they make you a simple spectator of your own movement.

I enter a second shop, smaller and more elegant than the first. The clothes on sale appear to be of good quality, but there is no price on them. This is embarrassing, also because as soon as I turn my eyes towards the tie section a slightly pushy assistant shows me half a dozen of them. On seeing I'm incapable of completing the knot on my own, she wraps one proficiently around my neck. She tells me that this tie is precisely the one that does for me. I look in the mirror. The pattern in the fabric seems too serious, perhaps dated. My face saddens, burdened by the heaviness of this noose, a hanging proboscis. Let us forget the ties. I thank the attentive assistant and leave. I have heard it said that shopping is an art, that some have developed the knack of "knowing how to shop" to the extent that they are summoned as "coaches" or experts for whoever has neither the time nor the ability to shop on their own. Negotiating one's way among the enchanted forest of the merchandise requires, according to some, a certain genius. My objective, in truth, was not to buy something to wear. I simply sought to offer myself a momentary distraction, to give some sense to my afternoon and to my solitude. Shopping would certainly allow me to return home with a memory, to take a photograph to send to my friends. For now I pick up again on my walk within the Quatre Temps.

The best of shopping is that, at least up until

the moment when the credit card has to be pulled out and payment made, this activity puts everything on the same level. Everyone is allowed to look, to try on the fine clothes just for a minute and to dream. But now the time has come to take a more courageous step, to attempt a more extreme experience. I head then towards the *sancta sanctorum* of the temple. I cross the threshold of a fast-food establishment. Yes, one of those belonging to the famous American chain. I had imagined it as a squalid place and, instead, I find with astonishment that even the most inferior of fast food outlets has undergone a process of aesthetic transformation. The clientele is mixed: from an unemployed man to a business woman and a student revising for a lesson. Everyone, however, is consuming the same drinks; they are all avidly eating the same french fries. Even the sandwiches, with the most varied names, all seem to the layman to be more or less the same. After all, the food on sale in this fast food outlet is intended for the universal, carbon-copy human being, the consumer without cultural or ethnic traits. If in the external world – in the troubled territory of the Parisian *banlieues* – the differences between groups of people are likely to be exacerbated, in the insulated fairy tale world of the Quatre Temps they are evened out through the display of conciliatory symbols. Some areas of the Parisian *banlieues* give the walking man the sensation of being in a sort of Far West, a battlefield wherein there is no law and no order. Here, instead, I have the illusion of being safe. The Quatre Temps is a fairytale castle, a creaking fortress, a crystal dream that could shatter to pieces around me.

Whoever ventures into the magical and mellifluous spaces of the shopping mall experiences, more or less consciously, a gradual distancing from the outside world and a weakening of their own identity. The super-place indeed offers the privilege of anonymity, releasing the individual from the burden of social obligations. This unusual form of solitude is, however, combined with the illusion of being always accompanied, connected with thousands of other people and overloaded by a system of signs that occupy and appease our senses. After all, the predominant idea behind building a super-place like Les Quatre Temps is to create a clean break with its surroundings, both visually and spatially, so that the new structure will stand out like an enchanted fortress in the middle of a desert. It seems to me, indeed, that the attractiveness of a shopping mall is to some degree proportional to the void it manages to create around itself, so that it appears as a total alterity: a potent symbol that excites the collective imagination and is the simulacrum of a utopia. On the one hand is the fortress-supermarket, a dazzling treasure-chest, icon of hedonism and objectified wellbeing. On the other is the degradation of the backdrop landscape, the broken sidewalks, the traffic and the dangerous *cités*, the old housing estates of Nanterre. If the contemporary city tends to be built through contrasts, the alterity of retail spaces becomes an aesthetic principle that dominates their design. What is missing at La Défense, however, and makes it still not much liveable, is precisely that typical intermingling of residences, businesses, offices, museums and public buildings that is characteristic of central Paris.

The spread of super-places expresses not just an economic necessity, but also a need of today's man. With the decline of political utopias and traditional religious and moral values, shopping has become a mass ritual that allows the public to forget the misery of their lives and express at the same time the euphoria of a material well-being. What people are looking for is primarily a "diversion", in the etymological sense of "turn [the gaze] elsewhere": to banish the worries of one's own mind, to enjoy a feeling of being dazed and oblivious. Super-places are an expression of nihilism, a denial of the world, and at the same time simulacra of an entirely immanent abundance, because they immerse us in the illusion of a perpetual and indefinitely replaceable present, the present of our own desires. It seems to me, therefore, after the end of the great metaphysical stories, that flânerie, if regarded as a purely recreational activity, has thus become a generalized approach, with life being conceived of by the majority as a succession of entertainments and distractions. From this standpoint, there is no doubt that shoppers or tourists are the descendants of Poe's man of the crowd. After all, a super-place like the La Défense quarter is a great spectacle that evokes and sums up the aspirations of modern man. A spectacle without promises, without meaning, but one that distracts and occupies our minds, converting them to the cult of an illusion.

12.

Paris spleen

Boulevard de Bonne-Nouvelle

The symptoms became clearer every day. I remember one morning in February a few years ago. I was walking along the Boulevard de Bonne-Nouvelle, wandering aimless through the city. I was looking at the grand buildings and the shop windows in succession along the way. There was a cold drizzle harrying my face, while the sun appeared sporadically, pale, behind a veil of clouds. I was febrile, drifting. I'd left my job just a few days previously and, without knowing what I was looking for, I walked the arc of the boulevards of the Right Bank: from République to the Madeleine, from the Madeleine to République. Why I had fallen into that state, I couldn't say. Perhaps another person would have looked for an explanation. But I let myself be happily rocked, cynically complacent, by the lure of this new life without plans.

Whether or not I had a girlfriend, a family, a job, or whether I saw friends was of little importance in that moment. The world that surrounded me, my life and my future, it all seemed swallowed up in the same swamp. I was now developing an intolerance for Paris, but without managing to free myself from the vortex that this very city had created around me. The symptoms, as I was saying. At first they were slight: a feeling of progressive distancing from others and then of disgust for "common sense", for ordinary thought. An angst regarding my habits, the mechanical repetition of acts. And then the vague desire for a new life, for a remoteness. I forced myself to stay at home, in isolation, to meditate on a way out. But my body would not remain still, it forced me to go out. As soon as I was down there on the street, without a destination, I loathed the confusion of the city and wanted to return to my four walls. I found myself more than once walking in circles, and so my days were locked to this unwholesome roundabout. Flânerie had become a bad habit, an illness.

It was then that I fully understood the meaning of that expression used by Baudelaire: "the Paris Spleen". The life I was leading brought no progress, no teaching – it was a melancholy passing of time, the awareness of the chasm that existed between me and the world. That was how that February was, and I wandered aimlessly, free of commitments, without material constraints. While the rain fell unheeding on the shining façades of the Boulevard Haussmann and on the fake faces of the passers-by, sagging like so many cardboard masks, I penetrated step by step into the labyrinth of the dominant thought, of the illness. Thus these lines from *Les Fleurs du mal* returned to my mind:

> Every day we descend a step further toward Hell,
> Without horror, through gloom that stinks.

One of those phrases that you study in school and at the time they seem perfectly sonorous, but nothing more than literary ravings. But then in a precise moment, all of a sudden, they spring from memory and you understand exactly what they mean. The descent into the abyss with eyes wide open, without horror — that was what was happening to me.

Then I heard the discourse of people in the street, in the lecture halls, in the cafés. I read the titles of the films and the headlines of the newspapers. I debated with my friends and colleagues from back then. I had the clear feeling that Paris was seeking to lose itself, that the very civilization of which the French capital was the guiding light now wanted to let others take over and vanish. And I felt I was a sacrificial victim of this collective madness, also condemned to fall into the chasm. I saw people asleep, bewitched by the new superstitions. Paris was a ship of fools, it was a vessel taken over by some inebriate, frivolous man. It seemed to me that in the sense of fatigue, even of weakness developed by the city, together with its individualism and its uncontained hedonism, my sentence had also been modeled. Until one day I found the strength to pull myself out of this collapse. Not all the bodies were condemned and destined to the fall. I had found a way to resist and to escape gravity. It was the day I decided to leave.

When the times are objectively hostile, and you realize you are rowing against the current, with blind obstinacy, to the point of exhausting all your strength; when the things you love have been devalued or scorned by most people, and you haven't been cunning enough to find yourself a place in the winners' circle; when the weight of the superego is crushing and the chosen city is populated with portents to saturation point, then you understand that the moment has come to leave. Once places have been inhabited, they store the traces of everything you have lived and they will never be as they were before. Paris had become an unhealthy hovel. The plot of this city had exhausted, for me, its charge of inspiration and of mystery. Its crowds were no longer that nebulous and aquatic mass of humanity in which I loved to immerse myself. Now when I walked the streets I was afraid of being taken for a bandit, or worse, bumping into some bore or someone who knew me. The city was waterlogged in signs and memories. I understood that the flâneur has to manage, when the time comes, to free himself of Paris. He has to *know* how to leave. The man fleeing from himself will strive, after all, towards an ever more remote horizon.

There certainly exists a Parisian dream that is still alive and is constantly renewed, a mirage that reverberates among the books and in the collective imaginary. You will find it, this dream, among travel agents' advertisements, in the newspapers, and perhaps in some university publications. The myth doesn't die easily. It seems so eternal that the Parisians themselves live and nourish themselves on greatness past, they are arrogantly proud of it. Unfortunately, however, it's enough to take a walk towards Les Halles, step into the airport or arrive in the city through the Gare du Nord to understand that the reality of today's Paris is very different and distant from that dream.

The practice of flânerie spread during the nineteenth century, right here in Paris. It was invented not by tourists, but by the Parisians themselves, who had developed a particular relationship with public space, imagining the roads, the squares and the streets as "interior" places, like the rooms of a house to be lived in. If elsewhere the solitary walking man was a marginal individual, in modern Paris he became the real master of the streets. With the invention of the *passages* first of all and then with the opening of the grand avenues and the creation of the sidewalks, there came the birth of a homogeneous and suitable urban space for the practice of flânerie. The city of Paris was the living manifesto of modernity; it was a grand atelier for refining one's aesthetic sensibility and experiencing new forms of art. Today Paris has changed radically. It has become the museum and the simulacrum of its past. It has lost its harmony, its uniqueness, its splendor. And yet, even at its sunset, it still retains something grand.

The French capital today can no longer be the Promised Land of the flâneur. But it still is the cradle of the discipline, the sacred place that every flâneur must bear in mind and visit, just as all philosophers, at least once in their lives, make the pilgrimage to the ruins of Athens. The atmosphere of Paris is very particular and still manages to charm and amaze its visitors. The typical character of Paris, its *genius loci*, is a strong influence on the lives of those who live here. It is to be found not only in the monuments and paintings, in the fashion shops and in haute cuisine restaurants. It's an impalpable sign and at the same time it's something more profound. Whoever remains in Paris for a considerable stretch experiences, in a more or less conscious and more or less marked way, a change in the direction of their own lives. Every Parisian is gradually influenced, for better and for worse, by the city's character. I say this on the basis of my own experience, but also on that of other people who have chosen Paris, as I did, to nourish their own selves on its history and its culture.

Paris taught me to appreciate life and enjoy beauty. It has taught this to many people. But for a long time I have had the sensation that this city, so saturated, so competitive, and in some respects in decline, had condemned me and my peers to basking in the sterile quest for aesthetic pleasure. It was a life made of moments. It was a life without a destination. Flânerie had become, in the widest sense, an existential stage. Paris is the ideal city for dedicating oneself to bad habits, to dissipation. Many delude themselves that the show is eternal, others have even found fortune, have flourished in the swamp. Paris is, above all, a grand city of culture, but it is so for those who wish to remain spectators, "receivers" of things done by others. Whoever aspires to creating something new would instead do better, today, to go elsewhere.

13.

Epilogue - At the gate

Charles de Gaulle Airport

> *"Why come to Trude?" I asked myself. And I already wanted to leave. "You can resume your flight wherever you like" they say to me, "but you will arrive at another Trude, absolutely the same, detail by detail. The world is covered by a sole Trude which does not begin and does not end. Only the name of the airport changes."*
>
> (Italo Calvino, *Invisible Cities*)

The Generic City resembles Shenzhen, which resembles New York City, which resembles the City of London, which in its turn resembles Shenzhen and so on. The Generic City is rich in history. It presents itself as an encyclopedia, a "summary" of the known world. It has a strangely familiar appearance. You will always find the little kiosk that sells English-language business magazines and your favorite chocolate snacks. You will find a coffee shop serving "latte", "espresso" and "cappuccino". You will find a souvenir and gift shop where you can buy a classic French perfume. In the air you will hear the music of the pop group of the moment. The Generic City is always up-to-date and new. The Generic City resembles a big airport.

I arrived three hours early. I know a wait like that seems like time wasted, but that's the way I am – I like to take a taxi very early, to arrive at the terminal when the check-in desk is not yet open and to find myself a quiet place to one side and to wait. I like observing the people arriving and departing and imagining the stories of their lives. I like observing the shapes and the colors of the suitcases and watching the families struggling to push these burdens before them, or to drag them behind, with varying gestures and movements that display varying degrees of elegance. I like observing the behavior of people as they stand in line and to read in their eyes the hopes and the sadnesses of their lives. I like carrying out comparative analysis of the different uniforms and the stockings of the flight attendants. I like arriving early because that way I can listen to the passenger announcements and savor with a shiver the booming of the loudspeakers in the immensity of the hall.

At the check-in desk of my airline there are no longer any employees. One has to stand in line, insert one's details into a machine, print the ticket on one's own and attach the label to the luggage. Then a second line to deposit the burden on a conveyor belt. A mechanical voice invites you to weigh the case – "Good morning! Please … " Immediately afterwards you go through to security and the metal detector. As soon as you come out of the security area an enormous waiting hall opens up, constellated with boutiques. The lights are cold, the décor ascetic and geometrical. Even the smallest details are not random – it all corresponds to a calculation of functionality and cost saving. I feel that strange happiness that comes over me when I find myself in spaces that are completely "modern" and "international", in an architecture that is timeless and placeless. The airport is a utopian space. The chaos and the dirt of the city are now a distant memory. I would even be tempted to enter the fashion boutiques, not so much to shop, but more to steep myself even further in this cotton wool dream. But I choose to sit down and write a few messages with my cellphone.

Still two hours to go. I am sitting in front of my gate. The other passengers arrive gradually. Some sort out their earpieces, some hold their tablets, displaying a certain nonchalance, almost a detachment from this place and this present time. It is precisely this general apathy that stimulates in me some uneasiness. It is not clear to me, to be honest, whether I am returning home or setting off. I check nervously, several times, that I have all my documents with me and verify that the flight is not delayed. At a certain point, however, a man roughly thirty years old breaks the silence and starts singing a bit. He is clearly drunk and next to him he has a small rucksack and a bottle of liqueur bought at the duty free shop. It is almost completely empty. He must have sunk it down in a rush. He sings in Portuguese, a rather romantic song. The people near him move away prudently by a few meters. The man continues singing. After some ten minutes the police intervene. Two of them ask for his documents, but he says he remembers nothing. He stands up, sways and improvises an absurd dance. Another two policemen arrive, one of whom has a dog on a leash. They ask him his name. The man does not reply. Near the bottle of liqueur there is his boarding card, but no passport. He must have lost it. They take him away.

It would be nice to manage, even just for a single day, to forget myself. Travelling should be a form of escape from stress, a getaway. And yet in this very moment I feel more than ever that I am myself. Standing now, in the queue to board the aircraft, I hold my boarding card and passport firmly in my hand. Now we are all lined up, staring at the person in front of us or the screen of our phones and we drag our baggage. We look like the condemned before the gates of Dante's *Inferno*. Here we are finally before the latter-day Minos who takes our passports, assesses our souls and divides us in First, Business and Economy class. We enter the covered passage that leads directly to the plane and we start peeking at the boarding cards of the other passengers to discover who will be sitting next to us. What is waiting for us is not hell, nor is it a punishment. A man who is able to travel is not yet completely finished.

An airport waiting lounge – would this be the culmination, the destination of my flânerie? If it is true that every consumer experience today includes a journey, then, conversely, a journey has become the consumer experience *par excellence*. Nowadays everyone travels – it is the true mania of our times. We travel for work, to take a break, to go study, to get away, out of despair or simply as something to do. This frenetic physical transfer is accompanied by an eagerness to record and furnish evidence of one's own adventures. As such, we are overwhelmed with photos and videos of travels on social networks, to the extent that the true rebel today is someone who manages to stay shut away at home and doesn't move. Like all the children of this restless generation, I too am a victim of this mania for travel: waking up early and braving the taxi or train ride to the airport weighed down with luggage; crossing the boutique-filled concourses, negotiating the security controls, checking in and proving my identity. And then, after hours of flying, arriving at an airport in another city, Beijing for example, only to find the same shops, the same soft drinks and perfumes and then repeating the same actions in reverse to pick up my luggage and finally achieve my freedom once more. And if in Paris I was looking for Beijing, in Beijing I will end up looking for Paris, longing for a crusty baguette, a painting by Courbet, an Italian shirt. In this sense, it is tempting to agree with Augé who says that travel as an experience of discovery, as understood by the anthropologists and explorers of the past, has become impossible today.

The tourist's journey – perhaps this, conceptually, is the exact opposite of flânerie. The tourist is an individual who moves his body without ever really departing. And yet the flâneur too may travel or depart. The same quest he engages in on the streets of Paris can be applied to various landscapes – to one, a hundred, a thousand other cities. At this point I could perhaps say, putting Huart's quotation back to front, that the flâneur was born in Paris, but he could live, today, in any other place. Indeed the flâneur indicates another life, a different way of getting to know the world. I have often heard it said that all places are the same, that travel serves no purpose because wherever you go you take yourself along with you and because it is only the sky that changes, not the souls of those traveling to cities or faraway lands. But I think this is far from the truth: I believe there really is a *genius loci* specific to each city – even to every district and every street – a little devil who gradually sneaks inside us to guide our habits and ideas and even to determine the course of our lives. The flâneur stalks this impalpable force. He, who knows how to recognize a road by its smell – and remembers what happened on a specific date in a certain street as if he had been there himself – he walks familiar places with constantly renewed excitement. The city remains a *terra incognita*, theatre of unpredictable interactions and influences. So even a shopping mall, even a parking lot or the drabbest of suburbs, are mines of stories and opportunities that can reveal themselves only to him. For those able to read the poetic text of the city, every place is infinitely rich; banality does not exist.

I finished writing this book in Beijing in April 2017.

Memorandum for flâneurs

1. You must move through the city at random – left or right with no reason, with no destination.

2. Ignore the tourist guides. Forget the stereotypes, the nonsense you've seen on television or read in the newspapers.

3. Escape from the banality of everyday life. Escape from the memories and the ghosts of the interior life.

4. Reject the rules of production and consumption. Consecrate your life to the moment, to ephemeral things.

5. Train your eye – unmask the superficial in the profound, spot the profound in the superficial.

6. Train your body – keep going for several hours while drifting without nourishment and without rest.

7. Listen to the voice of the world – immerse yourself in external reality to the point of becoming one with it and, ultimately, vanishing.

8. Abandon yourself to the crowd. Make the most of anonymity, of the sensation of emptiness and impunity that the big city can provide.

9. Do not neglect the suburbs, the anomalous and marginal spaces. Walk the streets that a tourist would never take.

10. Feel yourself to be free, open to the imponderable. Don't lose your way, lose yourself in the city streets.

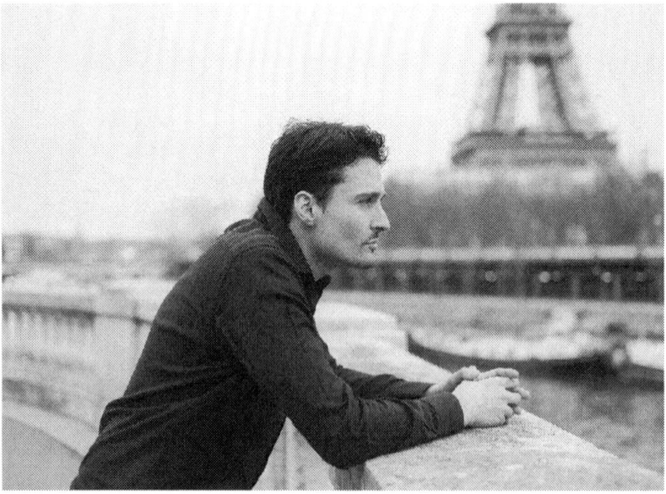

BIBLIOGRAPHY

Books

Aldéguier 1826 — ALDEGUIER, Jean Baptiste August d', *Le Flâneur. Galerie pittoresque, philosophique et morale de tout ce que Paris offre de curieux et de remarquable*, Paris, Chez tous les marchands de nouveautés.

Apollinaire 1993 — APOLLINAIRE, Guillaume, *Le flâneur des deux rives* (I ed. 1918), Paris, Gallimard.

Aragon 1953 — ARAGON, Louis, *Le paysan de Paris* (1926), Paris, Gallimard.

Balzac 1996 — BALZAC, Honoré de, *Physiologie du mariage* (1829), Paris, Gallimard.

Balzac 2000 — BALZAC, Honoré de, *Facino Cane* (1837), Paris, Éditions La Longue vue.

Balzac 2002 — BALZAC, Honoré de, *Ferragus, chef des Dévorants* (1834), Paris, Gallimard.

Baudelaire 2003a — BAUDELAIRE, Charles, Écrits sur l'art (1845-1869), Paris, Librairie générale française.

Baudelaire 2003b BAUDELAIRE, Charles, *Petits poèmes en prose: le Spleen de Paris* (1869), Paris, Gallimard.

Baudelaire 2008 BAUDELAIRE, Charles, *Les fleurs du mal* (1857), Paris, Gallimard.

Breton 2007 BRETON, André, *Nadja* (1964), Paris, Gallimard.

Calvino 1972 CALVINO, Italo, *Le città invisibili*, Torino, Einaudi.

Daeninckx 1993 DAENINCKX, Didier, *Autres lieux*, Paris, Verdier.

Daeninckx 1994 DAENINCKX, Didier, *En marge*, Paris, Gallimard.

De La Bretonne 1986 DE LA BRETONNE, Rétif, *Les Nuits de Paris* (1788-1789), Paris, Gallimard.

Fargue 1948 FARGUE, Leon-Paul, *La Flânerie à Paris*, Paris, Commissariat général au tourisme.

Fournel 1867 FOURNEL, Victor, *Ce qu'on voit dans les rues de Paris*, Paris, Dentu.

Hallberg 1996 HALLBERG, Ulf Peter, *Flanörens blick: en europeisk färglära: roman*, Stockholm, Norstedts.

Hessel 2011 HESSEL, Franz, *Spazieren in Berlin* (1929), Berlin, Verlag Berlin-Brandenburg.

Huart 1841 HUART, Louis, *Physiologie du flâneur*, Paris, Aubert.

Huysmans 2014	HUYSMANS, Joris-Karl, *À rebours* (1884), Paris, Flammarion.
Le Flâneur 1806	*Le Flâneur au salon ou M. Bon-Homme: examen joyeux des tableaux, mêlé de vaudevilles*, Paris, M. Aubrey.
Mercier 1979	MERCIER, Louis Sébastien, *Tableau de Paris* (1781-1788), Genève, Slatkine.
Paris 1831	*Paris ou Le livre des cent-et-un*, Paris, Ladvocat.
Perec 1998	PEREC, Georges, *Un homme qui dort* (1967), Paris, Gallimard.
Perec 2000	PEREC, Georges, *Espèces d'espaces* (1974), Paris, Galilée.
Perec 2008	PEREC, Georges, *Tentative d'épuisement d'un lieu parisien* (1982), Paris, Christian Bourgois.
Poe 1975	POE, Edgar Allan, *Complete Tales & Poems* (1832-1849), London, Vintage books.
Queneau 1980	QUENEAU, Raymond, *Courir les rues*, Paris, Gallimard.
Réda 1988	RÉDA, Jacques, *Recommandation aux promeneurs*, Paris, Gallimard.
Réda 1990	RÉDA, Jacques, *Le Sens de la marche*, Paris, Gallimard.
Réda 1993	RÉDA, Jacques, *Les Ruines de Paris*, Paris, Gallimard.
Réda 1997a	RÉDA, Jacques, *La liberté des rues*, Paris, Gallimard.

Réda 1997b	RÉDA, Jacques, *Le méridien de Paris*, Paris, Fata Morgana.
Réda 2001	RÉDA, Jacques, *Accidents de la circulation*, Paris, Gallimard.
Rolin 1995	ROLIN, Jean, *Zones*, Paris, Gallimard.
Rolin 2002	ROLIN, Jean, *La Clôture*, Paris, Gallimard.
Rousseau 1972	ROUSSEAU, Jean-Jacques, *Les rêveries du promeneur solitaire* (1782), Paris, Gallimard.
Sinclair 1997	SINCLAIR, Iain, *Lights Out for the Territory*, London, Granta.
Sinclair 2002	SINCLAIR, Iain, *London Orbital*, London, Granta.
Soupault 1997	SOUPAULT, Philippe, *Les Dernières Nuits de Paris*, Paris, Gallimard.
Walser 2001	WALSER, Robert, *Der Spaziergang* (1917), Berlin, Suhrkamp.

Studies on the figure of the flâneur

Benjamin 1982 — BENJAMIN, Walter, *Das Passagen-Werk* (1927-1940), Frankfurt, Suhrkamp.

Castigliano 2012 — CASTIGLIANO, Federico, *Il detective e l'uomo della folla: il doppio volto del* flâneur *in* The Man of the Crowd *di Edgar Allan Poe*, in *Comparatistica e intertestualità*, a cura di SERTOLI, Giuseppe, VAGLIO MARENGO, Carla, LOMBARDI, Chiara, Alessandria, Edizioni Dell'Orso.

Castoldi 2013 — CASTOLDI, Alberto, *Il flâneur. Viaggio nel cuore della Modernità*, Milano, Mondadori.

Coverley 2006 — COVERLEY, Merlin, *Psychogeography*, Harpenden (Herts), Pocket Essential.

Keidel 2006 — KEIDEL, Matthias, *Die Wiederkehr der Flaneure*, Würzburg, Königshausen & Neumann.

Montandon 1996 — MONTANDON, Alain, *Promenades et écriture*, Clermont-Ferrand, Université Blaise Pascal.

Nesci 2007 — NESCI, Catherine, *Le flâneur et les*

	flâneuses. Les femmes et la ville à l'époque romantique, Grenoble, ELLUG.
Neumeyer 1999	NEUMEYER, Harald, *Der Flaneur: Konzeptionen der Moderne*, Würzburg, Königshausen & Neumann.
Nuvolati 2006	NUVOLATI, Gianpiero, *Lo sguardo vagabondo. Il flâneur e la città da Baudelaire ai postmoderni*, Bologna, il Mulino.
Parsons 2000	PARSONS, Deborah, *Streetwalking the Metropolis*, Oxford, Oxford University Press.
Solnit 2000	SOLNIT, Rebecca, *Wanderlust: a History of Walking*, New York, Penguin.
Tester 1994	TESTER, Keith, *The Flâneur*, New York, Routledge.
White 2001	WHITE, Edmund, *The Flâneur*, London, Bloomsbury.
Wilson 1992	WILSON, Elizabeth, *The invisible Flâneur*, «New Left Review», 191, pp. 90-110.

Studies on Paris and other works cited

Agnoletto et al. 2007	AGNOLETTO, Matteo, DELPIANO, Alessandro, GUERZONI, Marco (eds), *La civiltà dei superluoghi*, catalogue of the Bologna exhibition (13 October – 7 November 2007), Bologna, Damiani.
Augé 1992	AUGÉ, Marc, *Non-lieux*, Paris, Édition du Seuil.
Augé 1997	AUGÉ, Marc, *L'Impossible Voyage*, Paris, Éditions Payot & Rivages.
Augé 2003	AUGÉ, Marc, *Le temps en ruines*, Paris, Galilée.
Bailly 2001	BAILLY, Jean-Christophe, *La Ville à l'œuvre*, Besançon, Les Éditions de l'Imprimeur.
Bataille 1957	BATAILLE, Georges, *L'Érotisme*, Paris, Minuit.
Baudrillard 1981	BAUDRILLARD, Jean, *Simulacres et simulation*, Paris, Galilée.
Bauman 1997	BAUMAN, Zygmunt, *Postmodernity and Its Discontents*, Oxford, Blackwell.
Benjamin 1955	BENJAMIN, Walter, *Charles Baudelaire.*

	Ein Lyriker im Zeitalter des Hochkapitalismus (1914), Frankfurt, Suhrkamp.
Castells 1996	CASTELLS, Manuel, *The Rise of the Network Society, The Information Age: Economy, Society and Culture*, Cambridge (Massachusetts), Blackwell.
Castigliano 2010	CASTIGLIANO, Federico, *Le divertissement du texte. Écriture et flânerie chez Jacques Réda*, «Poétique», 167, pp. 461-476.
De Certeau 1990	DE CERTEAU, Michel, *L'invention du quotidien*, Paris, Gallimard.
Debord 1988	DEBORD, Guy, *La société du spectacle* (1967), Paris, G. Lebovici.
Dictionnaire 1808	*Dictionnaire du bas langage*, Paris, Hautel.
Eco 2003	ECO, Umberto, *Dalla periferia dell'impero*, Milano, Bompiani.
Fournier 1855	FOURNIER, Edouard, *Paris démoli, mosaïque de ruines*, Paris, A. Aubry.
Giddens 1991	GIDDENS, Anthony, *The Consequences of Modernity*, Stanford, Stanford University Press.
Harvey 1989	HARVEY, David, *The Condition of Postmodernity*, Oxford, Blackwell.
Ilardi 2007	ILARDI, Massimo, *Il tramonto dei non luoghi*, Roma, Meltemi.
Kierkegaard 1923	KIERKEGAARD, Søren, *Enten – Eller* (1843), København, Nordisk Forlag.
Koolhaas, Mau 1995	KOOLHAAS, Rem, MAU, Bruce, *The Generic City*, in *Small, Medium, Large,*

	Extra-Large, New York, The Monacelli Press, pp. 1248-1264.
Lehan 1998	LEHAN, Richard, *The City in Literature, an intellectual and cultural History*, Berkeley, University of California press.
Leroy 1999	LEROY, Claude, *Le mythe de la passante*, Paris, PUF.
Mitchell 1995	MITCHELL, William, *City of bits*, Cambridge (Massachusetts), The MIT Press.
Monselet 1858	MONSELET, Charles, *Les Ruines de Paris*, Paris, L. de Potter.
Olsen 1986	OLSEN, Donald, *The City as a Work of Art*, New Haven (Connecticut), Yale University Press.
Pollock 1995	POLLOCK, Griselda, *Vision and Difference: Femininity, Feminism and the History of Art*, London, Routledge.
Sadler 1998	SADLER, Simon, *The Situationist City*, Cambridge (Massachusetts), The MIT Press.
Sansot 2004	SANSOT, Pierre, *Poétique de la ville*, Paris, Édition Payot.
Shortell, Brown 2014	SHORTELL, Timothy, BROWN, Evrick (eds), *Walking in the European city: quotidian mobility and urban ethnography*, Surrey, Ashgate.
Stierle 1998	STIERLE, Karlheinz, *Der Mythos von Paris. Zeichen und Bewusstsein der Stadt*, München, Deutscher Taschenburg Verlag.

Venturi et al. 1972   VENTURI, Robert, SCOTT BROWN, Denise, IZENOUR, Steve, *Learning from Las Vegas*, Cambridge (Massachusetts), MIT Press.

Webber 1964   WEBBER, Melvin, *Explorations into urban structure*, Philadelphia, University of Pennsylvania Press.

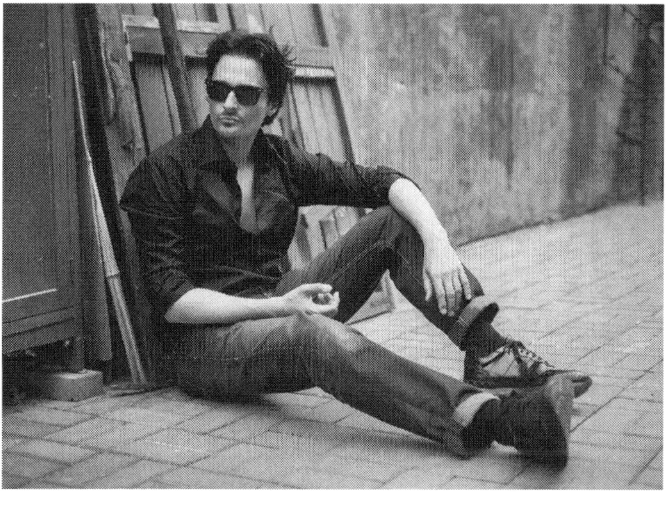

About the author

Federico Castigliano holds a PhD from the University of Turin (Italy) and is Associate Professor in Italian Studies. He worked for eight years in France (University of the South, Toulon-Var, University of Clermont-Ferrand, University of Nantes) and was part of a research team at the University of Paris (Sorbonne). Currently he teaches Italian language and culture at Beijing International Studies University in China.

He has written many essays and has read papers at conferences in several European universities. His first publications dealt with Italian cultural identity and Ligurian writers. During his years spent in Paris his research interests turned towards French culture, investigating the relationship between literary text and urban spaces.

Attracted by the Far East, in 2014 he moved to China, where he dedicates himself to writing works of fiction and autobiography. *Flâneur*, published in English in 2016, recounts episodes of flânerie and urban adventures in a Paris suspended between historical memory and "generic city". In 2017 the Italian translation of the book was published, just before the publication of the second English edition. In Beijing the author has played a leading role in several artistic performances, such as the experimental walks along the highway ring roads that surround the city.

Acknowledgments

With thanks to Dr Alberto Piatti for editing the Italian text, Architect Isaia Pruneddu for the design of the book, Prof. Iain Halliday for the English text. Thanks to my parents for their constant support and encouragement; and to my colleagues and students at Beijing International Studies University, who "contaminated" me with their enthusiasm and optimism. Finally, I thank all those who have accompanied me through these years of work and flânerie.

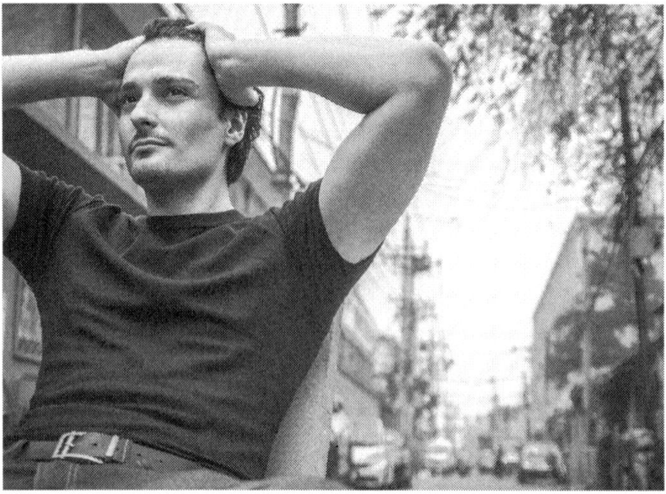

federicocastigliano.com

NOTE

NOTE

NOTE

NOTE

Printed in Great Britain
by Amazon